To Tom
Good Luck!
Stu Voigt

Dave Osborn
# 41

Go VIKES!

# PRAISE FOR A TRADITION OF PURPLE

"Walter Mitty meets Will Rogers in Jim Bruton's *A Tradition of Purple*. Bruton is an unabashed, diehard, over-the-top Vikings fan who lived out his dream 40 years ago when trying out with the team. It was the start of a beautiful relationship. Bruton never met a Vikings story he didn't like, and his tales include many anecdotes even the most loyal braid-wearing, horn-blowing, face-painting fan of the purple warriors has not heard before. If you bleed purple, you will want to read *Purple*."

—Joe Schmit, President
Petters Media & Marketing Group

"Jim Bruton … has written a compelling book: *A Tradition of Purple*. Bruton weaves anecdotes and stories together in a seamless fashion that give the reader new insight into the football club—the men who run it and those who play the game.
"For Bruton, who once tried out as a placekicker for Norm Van Brocklin and Bud Grant, the Vikings represent a significant part of his life. His book helps readers to understand why."

—Dave Nimmer
Retired reporter and teacher

"There is certainly nothing of the sterile objectivity one might expect from a university instructor in Jim Bruton's entertaining look at the Minnesota Vikings. But the Vikings have not, it's clear, become the dominant sports franchise in the state of Minnesota by inviting cold, dispassionate analysis. Rather, they have been a lightning rod for the emotions of young and old who identify with their unique and collective representation of this state and its people. Jim's very personal look at the team, its history, and its legendary characters is an entertaining and worthwhile read, sure to draw out some of those feelings from anyone with even a passing interest in the Minnesota Vikings."

—Mark Dienhart, Ph.D.
Executive Vice President
Chief Administrative Officer
University of St. Thomas

# A TRADITION OF PURPLE

## An Inside Look at the Minnesota Vikings

### JAMES BRUTON

SportsPublishingLLC.com

ISBN-13: 978-1-59670-208-0

Publishers: Peter L. Bannon and Joseph J. Bannon Sr.
Senior managing editor: Susan M. Moyer
Editor: Laura Podeschi
Art director: Dustin J. Hubbart
Dust jacket design: Dustin J. Hubbart
Project manager: Kathryn R. Holleman
Photo editor: Erin Linden-Levy

Sports Publishing L.L.C.
804 North Neil Street
Champaign, IL 61820
Phone: 1-877-424-2665
Fax: 217-363-2073
www.SportsPublishingLLC.com

Printed in the United States of America

Library of Congress Cataloging-in-Publication Data

Bruton, James, 1945-
A tradition of purple : an inside look at the Minnesota Vikings / James
    Bruton.
      p. cm.
    Includes index.
    ISBN 978-1-59670-208-0 (hard cover : alk. paper)
    1. Minnesota Vikings (Football team) I. Title.
GV956.M5B78 2007
796.332'6409776579--dc22
                            2007021713

# CONTENTS

# FOREWORD

IF YOU ARE A VIKINGS' FAN, old or new, this is the book for you.

Jim Bruton has captured the essence of the Vikings. From the beginning, the fact that they took the name *Minnesota* Vikings had great appeal and acceptance to the state and beyond. Training camps at Bemidji and Mankato were open to the public and people from all over flocked to watch and bond with the team. We now have second- and third-generation families who have been imprinted with the Vikings.

There was a time before free agency and salary caps that you could build a team that could last for years. Dallas, Miami, Pittsburgh, Oakland, and Minnesota were always contenders with winning records. Most of the players played out their careers with one team.

Times have changed, the names and numbers have changed, the ownership has changed, but the spirit of the Vikings is the same.

This book is a collection of memories of how the Vikings were built and by whom. I'm grateful that I had an opportunity to be a part of Vikings' history as a coach, and you can look forward to reliving some of the Vikings' history incorporated in this book and remain a Viking for life.

# ACKNOWLEDGMENTS

I WANT TO EXPRESS MY DEEPEST GRATITUDE and appreciation to Bob Hagan, director of public relations, and Brad Madson, director of community relations, for the Minnesota Vikings. Their longtime experience with the Vikings and their solid commitment to assist me with *A TRADITION OF PURPLE* have made the project incredibly interesting, exciting, and most enjoyable.

Bob and Brad each opened doors for me within the organization and in the community, for which I am eternally grateful. Their positive and unwavering support for the book has been inspiring and encouraging throughout every step of the process. I could not have written it without them.

I also want to sincerely thank Bud Grant, legendary coach of the Vikings, whose initial advocacy and support for the book's mission and goals has assisted me in developing the major theme for the book's content. I also want to thank Bud for writing the book's foreword.

Further, I would like to acknowledge my special thank you to Mike Pearson, former vice president of acquisitions, and Laura Podeschi, whom I am proud to call my editor, at Sports Publishing. Without their support and magnificent assistance along the way, the book would not have become a reality.

Further, I would be remiss in failing to mention the former and current Vikings staff, players, coaches, fans, and community agency representatives who took time from their schedules to accommodate my requests for interviews.

Finally, my deepest affection and thanks go to my wonderful family, who continue to provide me with all of their wonderful love and support.

# INTRODUCTION

## TRUE TO THE PURPLE

I WAS 18 YEARS OLD when I walked onto the Vikings practice field and approached Norm Van Brocklin. The late morning was saturated with radiant sunshine and a cool crispness hung in the air—a typical fall day in Minnesota. The manicured grass I crossed still had some residue from the morning dew, but what made the walk noteworthy were the glistening white chalk lines and goal posts standing erect at each end. I had entered the world of professional football.

It was 1963. The Vikings had just concluded practice at Midway Stadium in St. Paul and were walking off the field of the old baseball park, home of the former St. Paul Saints, a Triple-A farm club for the former Brooklyn Dodgers now based in Los Angeles. In the fall, the stadium was transformed into the Minnesota Vikings' practice home.

I had sat at the stadium many days in the 1950s enjoying battles between the Saints and Minneapolis Millers, both of which held future stars of the major-league Giants and Dodgers. Years away from becoming franchises in the Twin Cities, the Twins and the Vikings weren't even a figment of my imagination then. And I was a long way from any conversation with "The Dutchman."

Van Brocklin, one of the greatest quarterbacks ever, was named head coach of the Vikings before their inaugural 1961 season. He was legendary to the football follower and a powerful general on the field both as a player and coach. Known for his quick temper and controlling leadership, he was on a mission to bring a championship to the northland.

He came with a historic reputation as a winner, yet struggled in the early years to bring respectability to the NFL's newest franchise. It didn't make a difference to the locals. He was Van Brocklin, former NFL great, head coach of the Purple, and that was all that mattered. Forget what Vince Lombardi was doing over in Green Bay, this was Viking country and The Dutchman was in town.

As I got closer to him I asked myself, "What in the world am I doing?" It was too late to turn back. I was almost there. I was walking straight for him. The chalk lines and goal posts had disappeared from my thoughts and everything seemed surreal. The moment had arrived.

I introduced myself and passionately said, "Coach, I can kick a football farther than anyone you have on the Vikings." The expression on his face told me it was not likely anyone had ever said anything like that to him before, certainly not some kid barely out of high school and definitely not some uninvited guest at a Minnesota Vikings practice session.

This outrageously bold yet confident statement had an initial impact on Van Brocklin. He seemed surprised and taken off guard by the remark. I was the more surprised, however, just being there and having completed my mission.

Van Brocklin was a giant in football circles. A fearless leader, he was known for his brilliance in signal calling and for his pure understanding of the game. Devising a game plan and dissecting a defense was a process of simplicity. He was a genius at it.

Don Joyce, the great Baltimore Colt who finished his celebrated career with the Vikings, speaks of Van Brocklin as a "brilliant coach" and "an expert in spotting weaknesses" in an opponent. The magnitude of knowledge Van Brocklin learned as quarterback throughout 12 NFL seasons prepared him well for the reins as a head coach. He was a technician and knew every detail of the game.

As a player, the Vikings leader spent his first nine years with the Los Angeles Rams before being traded to the Philadelphia Eagles. It was a great fit and took only three years for Van Brocklin to guide them to the championship. At the time, he was a future Hall of Famer and one of the most prolific passers in NFL history. He once lit up the opposition for 554 yards during a single game in the 1951 season.

A good day for an NFL quarterback is 300 yards. A great day is 400 yards. Under the incredible competitive conditions of a game in the NFL, 500 yards is obscene. That almost unfathomable game set the standard for excellence.

So there he was, the leader of the Purple, one of the most illustrious and toughest quarterbacks of all time, confronted by a brazen 18-year-old who had the audacity to walk onto the Viking practice field and make such a profound statement. I said it and I believed it.

Van Brocklin never stopped walking but was courteous enough to look me straight in the eye and say, "Call us in the spring and we'll find out." I remember the look he gave me, and every part of the expression on his face.

It was cold and it was deliberate but also sincere. He looked tired and worn out—too many pressures, too many collisions, too many hours of mayhem. If he would have said, "Get lost, kid," and yelled for security, it would have been all right. I had just talked to a football legend, former Ram and prominent Eagle Norm Van Brocklin. I thanked him and made that call in the spring. He said he would give me a shot, and he lived up to his word.

Growing up in the Twin Cities prior to 1961, we knew nothing of the Minnesota Vikings. They didn't exist. No professional football existed in the area. So what did a diehard, young football fan, or any fan for that matter, do in those days but, I am sorry to say, inherit a passion for the Green Bay Packers. And I did. I can't imagine it today after 46 years as a Purple faithful, but it was a reality at the time. I watched, I listened, I read, and I cheered for the Packers.

Listening to Ray Scott as he called the games and watching the Packers lose most every week was fairly common, at least until Lombardi landed in Green Bay. In the Twin Cities area on Sundays, living rooms were filled with Bart Starr, Paul Hornung, and Ray Nitschke. Boyd Dowler, Max McGee, Jimmy Taylor, and Willie Davis filled our fall weeks with the hope of winning. It rarely occurred. And about the time Lombardi began building his team, loyalties changed forever. The Minnesota Vikings were born and my colors changed to purple.

Professional football arrived in Minnesota like gangbusters and the beloved Vikings began their first season. The Purple faithful had high expectations, but no one could have predicted the inaugural launching. The Vikings opened the year against George Halas' Chicago Bears at Metropolitan Stadium in Bloomington, Minnesota. I was there to observe firsthand what some experts have called one of the greatest upsets in NFL history. The Bears' stunning and unexpected defeat was thought in NFL circles to be some sort of miracle, an unbelievable occurrence.

Who were these "Men of Purple" who had the audacity to not only defeat but soundly annihilate the Chicago Bears? They were unknown rookies, other teams' castoffs, and free agents. And they won with a head coach who had never coached a football game in his life, as well as, most surprisingly, a signal caller making his first appearance in a professional football game.

The Purple were led by an upstart first-year quarterback from the University of Georgia named Francis Tarkenton, who came off the bench to throw four touchdown passes and defeat the proud and mighty "Monsters of the Midway" 37-13.

It was more like a backward swim across the English Channel, a 100-mile run through Death Valley, a duffer shooting 62 at Augusta, or the conquering of Everest than it was an opening victory. The first-year, first-game Minnesota Vikings didn't just sneak out a last-second victory against the Chicago Bears, they obliterated them! They slaughtered them, devoured them, tore them apart, and beat the last grimace of a Chicago Bear into total and resounding submission.

When it was over and the 37-13 score settled on the giant scoreboard at Metropolitan Stadium, I'm not even sure Van Brocklin believed it had really happened.

The Viking ship landed that beautiful Sunday afternoon in Bloomington, Minnesota. The team was now 1-0 and had defeated the Chicago Bears. It was an incredible beginning and set the cornerstone for a franchise that has become a community icon throughout the years.

Spring came in 1964, and I made the call to the Viking office. The team lived up to Van Brocklin's promise and I met Lew Carpenter and Tommy McCormick, Viking assistant coaches at Bloomington High School, for an unofficial NFL tryout with the Minnesota Vikings.

It was a windy, warm afternoon and the football reacted like a balloon upon impact. It seemed to stay airborne forever. My right leg was more like a cannon that day, and when it was over I was told, "You were right, you can kick the ball farther than anyone we have." It was like a dream, only to be shattered by a regulation that ended any immediate hopes for a future in the NFL.

Unfortunately, NFL rules at the time prohibited any pro football team from signing any player until at least four years after he entered college. This meant a tryout was fine, but sign a contract? Not until at least 1967. It was disappointing, but I knew I would someday be back again.

The Vikings made a call to the University of Minnesota. It was greatly appreciated. I had a brief career at the university and the opportunity to play for Murray Warmath. I didn't play much—a couple of games against Indiana and Michigan and a lot of games against the freshmen. In high school I had a bone disease in my legs and found that kicking the football was a way to play, so the desire stayed past the university and on to several NFL free agent tryout camps.

In the spring of 1967 I went to Davenport, Iowa, to try out for the Dallas Cowboys. Their kicker had retired and they were on a mission to find a new one who could be with them for many years.

The Cowboys were traveling in two years to 26 cities in hopes of discovering a kicker. They called it the "Kicking Karavan," led by former NFL kicker Ben Agajanian. I finished first in Davenport and was told by the Cowboys to wait for a few more of their city stops, after which they might sign me. My patience was short-lived.

I came home and contacted the Vikings. I told them about Van Brocklin's promise and the Cowboys tryout. Within a short time, I received a call from Jerry Reichow, former Viking player and player personnel director. I will never forget his words: "Coach Grant would like to bring you to training camp. We will send you a contract in the mail."

It was Bud Grant's first training camp as head coach, but his accomplishments at the University of Minnesota were so legendary that the Purple fans accepted him before he coached his first game. The contract arrived. I signed it and began to prepare for training camp with the Minnesota Vikings.

I could never have kicked for the Cowboys anyway. I would have had to miss on purpose if we were playing the Vikings. How could I do anything to hurt the Purple? I probably would have had something in my contract allowing me not to dress for Vikings games. I suppose the Cowboys would have figured it out if I were to sit on the Vikings' side of the field.

I was in training camp a short time and got to meet the great kicker Fred Cox. Cox was a machine—one of the best kickers ever. I remember thinking once during practice, "How am I going to ever beat this guy out if he never misses?" During my observations, I never saw Fred Cox miss a field goal or an extra point. Not much of a chance for an inexperienced rookie.

In 1968 I tried again, this time in Chicago at a second "Kicking Karavan" tryout. I was signed by the Dallas Cowboys, but left training camp during the first NFL player strike to return to my job. When the strike ended, I chose not to return.

In 1971, I signed a contract with the Minnesota Vikings for a second time, only to once again watch Cox go unblemished in his field goal attempts. Fred Cox was a nice guy and real gentleman. It didn't seem to bother him that I was after his job again, because he treated me well and even helped me with technique. He had all the mechanics and the perfect disposition for the pressure inherent as a kicker in the NFL. He was a true professional and a great representative of the Purple. I have always been proud to know him. Fred played college ball at the University of Pittsburgh as a running back and kicker, and was recently elected to the University of Pittsburgh Hall of Fame.

Kicking field goals and extra points for the Purple was just not to be. My relationship with the Vikings came about another way. Last year, 2006, represented my 40 years as a season ticket holder, and it has been a great ride. The NFC Championships and four Super Bowls have brought memories to last a lifetime.

A friend and true sports zealot once told me that basketball, hockey, and baseball just get him through to the next Viking football season. I think he spoke for many of the Purple faithful.

I heard a weather forecast recently speak of a cold front moving into the area. *Webster's New Universal Unabridged Dictionary* defines cold in part as "having a relatively low temperature...having little or no warmth...feeling an uncomfortable lack of warmth... chilled."

I have my definition of cold, as do most Purple fans of several decades. Cold is walking across the old Metropolitan Stadium parking lot in 30 degrees below zero wind chill to watch the Vikings play the Green Bay Packers. Cold is running to the restroom at halftime to try to warm up any part of the body in front of the ceiling heaters. Cold is continually moving in your seat during the game, stomping your feet, and wiggling your fingers in a valiant attempt to survive the hours of misery. Cold is trying to separate dollar bills with frozen fingers to pay for a hot dog that freezes before you take a bite.

Survival gear, as some might call it, included large snowmobile boots, gloves, a snowmobile suit, hood, and cap. Underneath were such items as sweatshirts, long underwear, sweatpants, and anything else that would fit. Sitting in the car before the game was a task, walking to the game was gruesome, and trying to keep from freezing to death was an even bigger accomplishment. It didn't matter. It was Viking football and it was what we did back then. Wind, rain, sleet, snow, and bitter cold—it was all just part of being a Viking fan.

As a loyal follower, I have felt a tremendous responsibility to tell the storied past, present, and future of this historic franchise and all

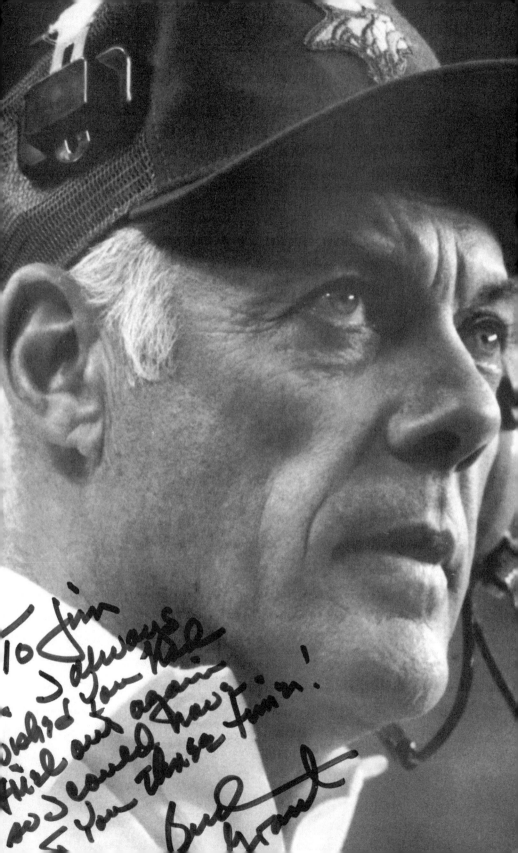

To Jim
I always
wished you well
& I could have
won those times!
Bud Grant

the tremendous accomplishments of the organization off the football field.

The Minnesota Vikings have used their iconic status the past 46 years to become valuable contributors to the community and people who deserve their assistance. This story has not been told. The incredible, meaningful relationships formed over the past several decades deserve mention and recognition.

This is an up-close look at an inspirational and wonderful organization with a big heart. The players, coaches, charities, Hall of Famers, front-office leaders, and behind-the-scenes faces come forth between these pages to give you an inside look at the Purple.

Norm Van Brocklin, Bud Grant, Fran Tarkenton, Carl Eller, Alan Page, Jim Marshall, and Mick Tingelhoff have been the names of this franchise for decades. Bill Brown, Dave Osborn, Stu Voigt, and the other great players who have lightened up our lives are all here to read about in the pages ahead.

With a lot of assistance from others, a fan—one who owns a picture of Bud Grant with the inscription, "Jim, I wish you would have tried out again so I could have cut you three times" as a prized piece of memorabilia and who once wore number 10 in Viking training camp before Fran Tarkenton wore it forever—brings you the Minnesota Vikings' story.

This is not a book about football, but a stimulating and inspirational inside look at an organization and what the enormity of its existence has meant to the community and region for the past four and a half decades.

THIS IS *A TRADITION OF PURPLE.*

Former longtime head coach Bud Grant continues to stand as the face of a proud Minnesota Vikings franchise. *Photo courtesy of the Minnesota Vikings.*

# 1

# THE DELIVERY ROOM

"I ALWAYS HAD THE FEELING at any time he might drop to the floor and do 100 push-ups. He was a wiry little guy who was very positive and full of energy," said Bill McGrane, Vikings public relations director from 1966 to 1972, of the Minnesota Vikings' original owner, Max Winter.

Max Winter saw his first NFL game in 1955 and was immediately in "awe" of professional football. It took little more than a glimpse of the action to instill in him the desire to become an NFL owner. Twenty-six years later in 1981, the headquarters and training facility of the Minnesota Vikings was named after him, dedicated as Winter Park.

His relentless passion for the game drove him to begin a crusade to bring professional football to the Twin Cities and the region. Prior to viewing his first game, Winter had been known locally as a Twin Cities entrepreneur. He was a restaurant owner, a boxing promoter, and the president of the famed hometown Minneapolis Lakers professional basketball team.

But it was professional football that really captured Max's interest in the late '50s, as he went on a persistent and nonstop pursuit to obtain a franchise. Some movement had been made toward granting Minnesota a team in the AFL, and he formed an alliance with other Twin City businessmen in this direction.

And there was a strong possibility that the local team would have originated in the AFL had it not been for George Halas, legendary owner and coach of the later-rival Chicago Bears. Halas wanted the Twin Cities in the NFL, and informed Winter of his support for the league to expand to the Northland. It wouldn't be easy, though, as some of the owners were not keen on expansion during the 1960s era.

The NFL owner meeting in Miami Beach, Florida, in January of 1960 kept the issue of expansion on the back burner for most of the session. Electing a new commissioner turned out to be the owners' major focus, and it wasn't until after the decision to elect Pete Rozelle to the post did the expansion issue surface toward resolution.

George Preston Marshall of the New York Giants was a major force against expansion, but finally acquiesced and voted with the majority, offering a motion for the conditions that would exist under which the new teams would enter the league.

After great patience by the local hopefuls, as well as behind-the-scenes dedication and hard work by Halas and others, an NFL franchise was awarded in 1960 to Minnesota and a group of owners headed by Max Winter. Other original owners were H.P. Skoglund, B.H. Ridder Jr., Bill Boyer, and Ole Haugsrud, who had been Winter's co-signer on the Twin Cities franchise application.

Haugrud, a likeable and friendly fellow from Duluth, was delivered a longtime promise by George Halas when the franchise was granted. The once owner of the Duluth Eskimos had been told he would have the chance to be a part of any new ownership when his professional football team ended its reign in 1922.

It took some four decades, but Haugsrud remembered the promise, as did Halas, and Haugsrud became a part owner of the new franchise. Although he didn't hold more than a 10-percent share, he still prided himself on being one of the initial owners.

On Friday, January 29, 1960, an article appeared in the *St. Paul Pioneer Press* entitled "DULUTH MAN HAILS MOVE," and read in part as follows:

"Ole Haugsrud of Duluth, co-signer of the Twin Cities NFL application with Max Winter, contacted in Spokane, Washington, en route home from a convention on the west coast, said:

"'Needless to say I am extremely happy over the announcement that Minnesota has been granted a franchise in the National Football League. I am sure this is only the beginning of a new era of major-league sports for Minnesota.'

"B.H. Ridder Jr., publisher of the *Dispatch* and *Pioneer Press*, said:

"'This is a very constructive thing for St. Paul and the Twin Cities and the granting of the franchise in the National Football League will lead to other major sports participation in the Twin Cities.'"

The plan was for the team to open its inaugural season in the fall of 1961, following Dallas' entry for the 1960 season. This NFL decision set the tone for future expansion in the years ahead. Halas, one of the most powerful owners and the biggest booster for expansion, was significant in convincing enough owners to follow his vision to grant Minnesota and Dallas entry into the league, the first teams to enter in a decade.

The Halas vote and support were influential in the decision to expand. The Twin Cities and the Minnesota team owed Chicago's "Papa Bear" a lot for his insistence on granting a franchise to the area, although they surprisingly paid him back in a rather uncomplimentary and noteworthy fashion.

Some might say it wasn't payment at all, and a sad way to repay such a grand debt. It certainly was not what anyone would cite as a "thank you." Others perhaps say the franchise was new and didn't understand how to pay back the great favor. There was no doubt that Norm Van Brocklin and his band of rookies and other team castoffs gave little thought to any kind of appreciation.

The new NFL entry showed its gratitude in the only way it knew, stomping the Bears 37-13 on the first day of its first season.

George Halas very likely never regretted his decision to support the Minnesota franchise entry into the league; however, it may be just as likely that, in the locker room shortly after the game, for a second he wondered what he had done.

It took what some described as perhaps the most significant change in NFL history when the owners passed an amendment to their constitution that allowed the league to expand if 10/12ths of the owners were in agreement. And the vote was there. Halas had won out in his support.

Expansion was also the first major decision made during the reign of the new NFL commissioner, Pete Rozelle, who had been elected by the owners as a sort of compromise candidate after days of snarling over potential new leaders.

Rozelle had been the general manager of the Los Angeles Rams and was elected to a three-year term as commissioner at the age of 33. His connection to Bert Rose, first general manager in Minnesota, also played a part in Rose coming to the Twin Cities to head up the new NFL organization in 1961.

The decision to expand the league from 12 to 14 teams was finally made. Max Winter had been waiting in the wings throughout the league meetings to see if the Twin Cities would be presented with a team. At one point, he had almost given up hope for a positive outcome.

Winter was 55 years old at the time and had advised the league that he was fully prepared to move quickly if awarded a franchise. He had several coaches in mind, a general manager picked out, and community support to the tune of guaranteeing 20,000 season ticket sales.

The *St. Paul Pioneer Press* reported headline news on Friday, January 29, 1960: "TWIN CITIES TO ENTER NFL IN 1961; DALLAS OK'D FOR '60" and "Marshall Votes With Majority."

The *Pioneer Press* article went on to read in part:

"St. Paul–Minneapolis and Dallas were granted National Football League franchises Thursday, the Texas city for 1960 and the Twin Cities for 1961.

Max Winter helped bring the Vikings to Minnesota in 1961.
*Photo courtesy of the Minnesota Vikings*

"NFL commissioner Pete Rozelle and the 12 owners also officially expressed sentiment for two more teams to be admitted within the next three years, creating two eight-team divisions.

"The new franchises were the first in the 40-year-old league since Baltimore, Cleveland, and San Francisco entered the circuit in 1950 from the old All-American Conference."

The organization was first known as Minnesota Pro Football Inc. Ole Haugsrud was named chairman of the board and Max Winter president and manager-director. E. W. Boyer and H.P. Skoglund, who had joined Winter in the now-surrendered AFL franchise, would also join with the new Minnesota team. Dan Williams of St. Paul was named vice president.

Although Winter held the team's title of president, Ridder and Skoglund possessed most of the power within the franchise in the early years. Winter would begin to take real control of the team and exercise some of the decision-making authority around the mid-'60s.

Skoglund was in the insurance business and was, along with the others, well liked. He and Boyer, a car dealer by trade, led the ownership with able and competent leadership.

Ridder was perhaps the most powerful with regard to his wonderful ability to command respect. He was a wealthy man, owning the *St. Paul* newspaper, and circulated in the highest of corporate circles.

Standing about 6 feet, 4 inches tall, Ridder also cultivated the ultimate in respectability from others. Jim Klobuchar, famed Twin Cities writer, described Ridder as "gregarious" and, as a side note, "a great golfer."

Klobuchar covered the Minnesota professional football team for many years as a sportswriter and later a columnist, and loved his early responsibilities with the men clad in purple. He was complimentary of the early ownership, stating the individuals were "very different in their backgrounds and personalities" but worked together in their capacity for approximately 10 years.

Although Skoglund, Ridder, Boyer, Haugsrud, and Winter owned the team, they became most responsible for creating and installing a true family atmosphere. They played their roles very well and rarely interfered with the football part of the business. That part was left up to Joe Thomas, the chief scout; Bert Rose, the general manager; and of course, The Dutchman, Norm Van Brocklin, who gained more and more power as the team matured into a force in the NFL.

Eventually Van Brocklin prevailed as the true face and leader of the franchise, and Thomas and Rose left. When Jim Finks arrived, however, things would be different. Van Brocklin and Finks got along very well for the most part, having mutual admiration for each other's accomplishments as former players.

Professional football became a reality in the Twin Cities and the surrounding region. The delivery room had produced the beginning of a passionate love affair that would reach into another century and travel over five decades.

During all these lengthy discussions about the local beloved NFL entry, it is difficult to believe that at one time the team was simply called the St. Paul-Minneapolis franchise, or the Minnesota Pro Football Inc. Imagine if one were to hear Chris Berman announce the final score, "Minnesota Pro Football Inc. 24, Chicago Bears 20," or "St. Paul-Minneapolis Franchise 20, Green Bay Packers 17."

The scores sound OK though, and the team's identity would soon be in place, destined to become a Midwest treasure. Its name would ring in the ears of the forever faithful and make them proud of their heritage. Always associated with the color purple, it was beautiful—and it all belonged to Minnesota.

And the baby out of the deliver room would be named ... the MINNESOTA VIKINGS.

The name can be traced and credited to Bert Rose, the first general manager of the franchise, and the original owners who approved Rose's recommendation. The following provides the logic and passion that went into the decision.

The *1961 Minnesota Vikings Radio, TV, and Press Guide* reads in part:

"When Bert Rose was selected as general manager, one of the first steps he took was to recommend to the board of directors that the club be nicknamed the 'Vikings.'

"'Certainly the Nordic Vikings were a fearless race. Following many years of victories in the British Isles and France, under Eric the Red, they sailed in open boats across the North Atlantic seeking new peoples to conquer. Their entire history is punctuated with the aggressive desire and will to win.'

"He convinced the owners and the rest is history."

Hub Meeds, "THE VIKING" who paraded the sidelines as the team's mascot for so many years, smiles as he speaks of the great Viking heritage and all the claims made on it. After being invited to take part in events, celebrations, and festivals with the Norwegians, Swedes, and Danes, all claiming the heritage, one can only praise the importance of the connection and its rich and proud traditions.

And so the franchise was born.

Prior to the arrival of the Purple, the only professional football in the area consisted of the Green Bay Packers, led by such names as Bart Starr, Paul Hornung, Boyd Dowler, Jerry Kramer, Ray Nitschke, and, of course, head coach Vince Lombardi. Of course, Gopher football had made its mark on the area with the great teams of the early '60s. The likes of Carl Eller, Bobby Bell, and Sandy Stephens had laid the groundwork with consecutive Rose Bowl appearances, but the Twin Cities wanted more.

Watching the autumn colors change in Minnesota is a beautiful sight. The reds, orange, and yellows engrained in the leaves on the trees and those falling to the ground make up one of the area's greatest seasonal enjoyments.

Sitting in a living room, den, family room, or maybe a garage in the late '50s and early '60s also brought some great colors of interest, as the green and gold of the Green Bay Packers became a Sunday tradition. Most of the football faithful never made the trip to Lambeau Field and most never saw a professional game in person. Watching the team go from perennial loser to big-time winner on television was fulfillment enough during those years, because another color was not even on the horizon.

And then the Purple arrived in the form of a team called the Minnesota Vikings, taking over and smothering its surroundings in a beloved, mutual admiration for almost half a century.

The cold backdrop of the Packers' homeland was replaced by a fixture they called Metropolitan Stadium, and soon those names that once filtered into living rooms on Sunday afternoons—Bart Starr, Paul Hornung, Boyd Dowler, Jerry Kramer, Ray Nitschke, and of course Vince Lombardi—were replaced with names like Hugh McElhenny, Tommy Mason, Mick Tingelhoff, Fran Tarkenton, Bill Brown, and Norm Van Brocklin. And they all wore purple.

The community embraced the team in a fashion so unusual, it was almost as if the wins and losses were accomplished together, with the team and the fans each playing their own significant roles. The celebrating and the suffering were as one. Maybe the old Metropolitan Stadium and the cold, wind, and snow of the Northland contributed to it. Either way, it was and remains something very special.

"The wind chill was 33 degrees below zero as I stood out on the field and looked up into the stands, and there wasn't an empty seat," said former Viking kicking great Fred Cox of one game. "Who in the world would be crazy enough to go to a game when it is 30 degrees below zero? Who would go to a game like that?"

The cold and wind—and often snow—Cox speaks about didn't make a difference to the hearty Purple faithful who understood that this was "Viking football." It came with the territory. It was something to relish, and fans took pride in the tradition that went with it.

Great defensive end and local legend Jim Marshall follows up on Cox's statement by saying, "When we went out on the field, we were playing for people who loved and appreciated us."

He further commented on the great fans who have endured the coldest of weather conditions: "We were there and we were paid to be there, but the fans, they paid to be there. They were with us through thick or thin, and it was a love affair."

The old Metropolitan Stadium housed the Vikings for over two decades.
*Photo courtesy of the Minnesota Vikings*

Marshall is very passionate when speaking of the Purple faithful and has a deep appreciation for the loyal and bold fans who braved the most dastardly of conditions to cheer for the Minnesota Vikings.

"We were their warriors," proclaims Marshall. "They were our 12th man."

Marshall also has great regard for the original Viking owners and speaks highly of Max Winter, the Boyers, Skoglunds, Ridders, and Haugsruds. He says they "treated the players very well and made everyone feel like part of a family."

Maybe it was the role of the fans who endured the cold in similar fashion to the Vikings on the sidelines. Maybe it was the fact that Bud, "The Old Trapper," as referenced by a local scribe, didn't allow the players heaters or gloves. And maybe it was the fact that the fans could identify with all of this, and always believed they were in it together.

No heaters, no gloves, and even occasionally short sleeves in the bitterest of cold created this special bond that has lasted from the beginning. The fans and the Minnesota Vikings, set apart from the rest, doing it together.

It wasn't just madness. It was a belief. Bud Grant especially believed in it, or at least he let everyone think he did. He told the legendary tale of Eskimos handling the cold in Alaska and a study that was done to try to understand how they could do it and why. It all seemed to make sense and gave the players a reason they could easily understand.

In Alaska, when experts worked on the Advanced Warning Systems, it was found that the Eskimos could sit on bulldozers in the freezing cold longer than anyone else. If Eskimos were assigned the jobs, the work was done faster because they did not have to take as many breaks and could essentially be in the cold for unusually long periods of time.

A study later revealed that no physical differences existed between Eskimos and others that allowed them to work like this in freezing temperatures. They were simply adapted to it. They had become acclimated to the conditions and had accepted them.

Bud believed that, by becoming accustomed to the cold, players would have a strategic advantage over other teams that could not adjust. And so, the Vikings played without gloves and heaters.

When asked to describe how the Vikings survived under the most perilous of conditions in those old days at the Met, Cox summed it all up by asking, "You mean you haven't heard Bud's Eskimo story?"

They called it football, freezing cold football, but it was the way of the Purple, and the area loved it. It formed a bond between the fans and the team that has strengthened as decades come and go.

So the great franchise of Minnesota, clad in purple, had its beginning. It came about in a delivery room full of rich businessmen who simply took a vote and said Minnesota would field a professional football team in the fall of 1961.

And as the colors became real and the name became legendary, the team took the field on September 17, 1961, for that first regular-season game against the Chicago Bears and the person who had championed for the Minnesota franchise, George Halas.

If the delivery room presented the franchise to Minnesota on that fateful day in 1960 at a Miami Beach hotel, then it was the transformed baseball field at Metropolitan Stadium in Bloomington, Minnesota, that completed the birth, as the Minnesota Vikings walloped the tradition-rich Chicago Bears by 24 points.

The Vikings represented the baby, and the fans were the parents. And the love affair grew in the hearts and souls of the faithful who follow the Purple, reaching four and a half decades later. The Minnesota Vikings came home from the delivery room to become a part of the Twin Cities family.

# 2

# THE ARRIVAL
# OF THE
# DUTCHMAN

"DO NOT GO INTO THE AISLE of the aircraft! Do not go to the restroom or visit anyone aboard the flight! If your hear someone in the aisle approaching your seat, pretend you are asleep!"

These unwritten rules were put in place and religiously followed after a particular group of people experienced "a bad day at work" when traveling home from the west coast in the early to mid-'60s. No business attire was donned during their trip. These passengers wore purple.

They called him The Dutchman. When he arrived in Minneapolis in January of 1961 to take the head coaching job with the newly formed Minnesota Vikings franchise, Norm Van Brocklin was perhaps the most recognized name in professional football. After all, just a year before he had quarterbacked the Philadelphia Eagles to the NFL Championship against Vince Lombardi's Packers.

Having never coached before, Van Brocklin was a surprising choice for the position, but his dominating leadership with the Eagles and his extensive knowledge of the game made him an attractive candidate.

Bert Rose, the first general manager of the Vikings, chose Van Brocklin to coach the team—to his own demise, as the two clashed one too many times. The Dutchman could lead and he knew football, but working for someone else was just not in the cards.

Rose had a theory that supported his decision to hire an individual with no formal NFL coaching experience. He felt that, if someone had extensive football intelligence, a thorough understanding of the game's Xs and Os, and was a great motivator, it would be enough.

Van Brocklin's reputation as a great leader with a tremendous will to win also led Rose to believe the coach would instill a "trust me, I'll lead you to victory" philosophy that would combat any lack of coaching experience. What he didn't know was that ultimately, Van Brocklin would not be able to work for the man who hired him, and the boss would be the one to leave.

Determining who would fill the head coaching position wasn't easy. Rose initially considered bringing in the successful coach of the Northwestern Wildcats, Ara Parseghian. For a number of reasons, this never worked its way into close deliberation among the decision makers.

Other names, such as Sid Gilman of the Rams, Nick Skorich of the Eagles, and the great Otto Graham of the Cleveland Browns, were brought up as potential head coaches for the Vikings, but Rose and the owners eventually settled on the leader of the world champion Philadelphia Eagles, Norm Van Brocklin.

His field leadership and incredible knowledge of the game attracted the most interest. Rose was convinced that few knew more about football than Van Brocklin, and certainly his name in itself would draw enough attention to establish early credibility for the newly formed franchise.

It worked. The Minnesota Vikings were going to be led into gridiron battles on Sundays by Norm Van Brocklin, championship quarterback and future Hall of Famer. The move was overwhelming and the Twin Cities were ready for the ride. Professional football and the NFL had arrived, and the Dutchman was in charge.

Whoever coined the phrase "there is something in a name" must have been thinking about the infant born in Eagle Butte, South Dakota, on March 15, 1926. It must have been written in the books at the time, "If you are going to name your son Norm Van Brocklin, he will become a quarterback in the NFL and the first head coach of the Minnesota Vikings. He will lead the Philadelphia Eagles to the NFL Championship and become one of the most famous names in all of sports." How could he do anything else with a name like NORM VAN BROCKLIN?

If someone were to come up and ask you who the leader of your football team is, wouldn't you want to say "Norm Van Brocklin"? Wouldn't you want to say "Van Brocklin did this" or "Van Brocklin did that"? The name has a resounding ring. Toughness, competitiveness, and greatness are built into it, and they all came with the package.

Now in his late 60s, a loyal fan of Van Brocklin can still remember walking up the runway for his first look at the Los Angeles Coliseum playing field. And there, warming up on the gridiron in front of him, stood one of the greatest quarterbacks who had ever played the game of football—Norm Van Brocklin.

That was over 50 years ago, but it seems like yesterday to Don Mooney as he gazes over the field with the rest of his scout troop, who are taking in their first NFL game. Don grew up near the Coliseum and heard the noises reverberating from its inside on Sunday afternoons. He listened for names like Bob Waterfield, Elroy "Crazy Legs" Hirsch, and Van Brocklin, who made up the mystique of greatness that he assumed belonged inside the walls likely never to be seen by his eyes. It added to the glamour as he imagined what was taking place in each game.

Because he did not spend hours devouring every aspect of the sports pages growing up, Don never let those idols behind the historic walls drown away among the names of other great players. He just knew who played inside the Coliseum every weekend in the fall.

In fact, it took Don a while to learn that a first name was attached to Van Brocklin, as it was just assumed he was named similarly to the great actors Van Johnson and Van Heflin. Once the name "Norm" was attached, he became separated from the rest.

When Van Brocklin is mentioned today, a kind of reverence follows. Don remembers the chill that went down his back as he looked out onto the playing field at immortality. At the time, he was a 12-year-old boy staring at the brilliance of the green grass and the white chalk lines beneath the The Dutchman's feet. Van Brocklin was a hero.

Record-producing years in the NFL established his reputation as a take-charge, ferocious competitor. In Van Brocklin's 12 years of play, a Sunday afternoon win was the only acceptable outcome of the week's preparation.

While quarterbacking the Rams, the athlete shared duties with the great Bob Waterfield for a time, yet Pro Football Hall of Fame records show he won passing titles in 1950, 1952, and 1954. It is hard to fathom the enormity of such records that established his greatness and superiority.

A master at understanding every aspect of the game with legendary attention to detail, Van Brocklin's strengths came from his incredible awareness of every situation and his fearlessness in attacking defensive formations. He also knew players. He knew their strengths and he knew their weaknesses. If a weakness was discovered in an opposing player or an opposition's defense, he attacked it like a wild animal smashing out of a cage to freedom.

Former Vikings coach Jerry Burns says Van Brocklin was a "tough guy" and a "fiery competitor." The two became friends when Van Brocklin called upon Burns in the early years as an offensive consultant. During the initial years of the franchise, the coaches often bantered and theorized over offensive philosophy.

Burns had established himself as one of the game's great offensive minds while at the University of Iowa. But becoming a friend and consultant to another offensive genius occasionally led to more than just discussions, plans, and observations.

At times, both coaches' passions for the game and internal, driving desires to move the football down the field were perhaps too much to haggle over in a friendly way. In fact, a long, heated disagreement about certain aspects of attacking defenses almost took them out into the darkness one evening.

Van Brocklin apparently wanted to settle the argument outdoors, but Burns decided it was better to just change his "whole philosophy of offensive football." As Burns says, "He wanted to take me outside and beat the %@%# out of me." At 6 feet, 2 inches tall and about 220 pounds, Van Brocklin was not one to reckon with once his fire and passion advanced from smoldering to a recognizable blaze.

"Fiery" may have been an understatement. The Dutchman wanted to win. Receiving sound advice from another football genius certainly assisted in the process, as long as it didn't distract from his way of thinking.

When the Vikings won under Van Brocklin, the celebrations seemed endless. Bob Lee, former Viking and Atlanta Falcons quarterback, recalls that the coach once directed everyone to go out on the town for a good time, all expenses on him. So elated after big wins, Van Brocklin often went to these pleasant extremes.

It was quite the opposite, however, after a loss. Fred Zamberletti, longtime Viking trainer and current senior consultant and team historian, remembers the trips back from the west coast after losing efforts. They were unforgettable and the plane rides home unpleasant, to put it mildly. Losing was not part of the head coach's agenda and defeat was not in his vocabulary.

"The trip back from San Francisco or Los Angeles took about six and a half hours in those days, and it was tough after a loss," said Zamberletti. "We used to sit in our seats and not get up to use the restroom for fear of running into Van Brocklin in the aisle. And if he started walking up the aisle, we would be sleeping when he got near our seats. It was just that way." No one wanted to be on the receiving end of Van Brocklin's wrath after a defeat.

The Vikings coach was driven to win and expected to do so at all costs. Players say that The Dutchman had a difficult time coping with poorly played games. His emotions too often got the best of him. Those who played for both Van Brocklin and later Bud Grant saw very different approaches to games in which victories didn't occur.

Grant believed that, for a team to be successful, all they had to do was win most of the time. Opponents would prevail at times because they were superior, or because they just played better on that given Sunday. He knew that other teams were getting paid to

Norm Van Brocklin (with chalk) and staff discuss a play.
*Photo courtesy of the Minnesota Vikings*

win, too, and could accept losses as long as they were significantly fewer than victories.

It was hard to determine from Bud's demeanor whether the Vikings were ahead or behind in a game. And at the end of a matchup, watching Grant would give little clue as to whether the Vikings had just won or lost. He was extraordinarily consistent, and understood the finite details of how to cope with victories and defeats.

Van Brocklin's character, on the other hand, could be described as interesting, alarming, challenging, and charming. He was adept at changing his personality and mood in an instant.

Fred Cox, a former great Viking kicker, recalls that Van Brocklin also discussed what had gone wrong with the game plan on each flight home after a loss. He wasn't afraid to tell players and anyone else in sight how he felt, and quite often showed his suffering for the duration of the trip. He spoke about the intricate details of the game over the mountains, on the take off, and even during the landing. Most of the discussions weren't pleasant memories of a vacation junket to the west coast, either.

Then, upon departure from the plane, his personality could change completely. Cox was one of few married players on the team, and his wife often met him at the airport with their 18-month-old son. On one occasion, as Van Brocklin departed from the plane and saw Fred's boy, the coach's mood swing was incredible. Mr. Rogers would have been proud.

Van Brocklin picked up the toddler and carried him all the way through the airport, talking and laughing with him, seemingly possessed with a passionate love for the little one. The earlier Viking loss had escaped from his radar screen in an instant flash.

During their time together, Cox remembers that the coach treated him in a professional and respectful manner. The kicker always felt that Van Brocklin was repaying him for a time when he had to release Cox due to a lack of roster space.

"I think I may have been the only player that Van Brocklin ever apologized to," says Cox. After being traded from Cleveland to the Vikings during preseason, Cox had a good camp. He was called in for a meeting after one game in which he had contributed two field goals and several kickoffs into the end zone. Van Brocklin told Cox he did a great job, but the coach only had 36 roster spots and could not afford to keep a kicker in one of them.

When the roster was increased to 38 the next year, Van Brocklin called him back, and Cox, after making five field goals in one game, became the Minnesota Vikings' kicker for the next decade and a half.

"He always treated me well and never had a cross word for me, and I believe it had to do with cutting me off the team due to the shortage of roster positions," says Cox. Others were not so fortunate, though, and found their time with the Vikings under Van Brocklin's leadership very trying.

Some say it simply and candidly. Norm Van Brocklin was a football genius but had difficulty handling people.

One former player stated, "I don't want to take anything away from Jerry Burns, because he was one of the greatest offensive coordinators that ever lived, but if The Dutchman was the coordinator under Grant, the Vikings would have won 10 Super Bowls."

After hearing this remark, another former player under Van Brocklin said, "I don't think so. Grant would have fired him in the first few weeks!"

When Van Brocklin left the Vikings and became coach of the Atlanta Falcons, two of his longtime friends traveled to Atlanta for the game. The Vikings won and both individuals waited for Norm after the game. He never showed. They later learned he went straight home. The loss to his former team was just too much to bear.

Fred Zamberletti describes Van Brocklin as "the most competitive person I have ever met. He was extremely intelligent and very demanding of the players."

As a head football coach, he took great pride in expecting as much from his players as he expected from himself. To ask for anything less would not have been The Dutchman's style. Unfortunately, most of his men were never going to be the remarkable player that he was—a difficult concept for him to accept. Few people in any profession ever enter that special circle of "greatness." But Norm was in and he wanted company.

"I always felt if you were going to pick one guy to put in an offense to win one game, the first guy I would go to would be Norm Van Brocklin," says Zamberletti.

Friends and players describe him as a man with an incredible memory many wish for and a great respect for the game. Unfortunately for some players, this memory was not an attribute, especially if they happened to be on the wrong end of an unpleasant happenstance during a crucial time in The Dutchman's profession.

He was very loyal and believed strongly in the word and its meaning. However, his "tough guy" trademark wreaked havoc on more than a few players. He created a great deal of fear that sometimes overrode respect, but perhaps internal bleeding was the real culprit when things went wrong.

Zamberletti says that, when Van Brocklin was in the building, "You could feel it. You could feel him coming through the walls." An incredible, powerful force seemed to exude from him. Maybe it was the legendary status and fame he had achieved as a heralded quarterback, or maybe it was the incredible knowledge he had for the game that made him so unusual. Maybe, from time to time, the fear factor would just raise its ugly head when games were going in the wrong direction. Whatever it was, it was real.

He seemed to take a strong liking for the veterans and treated them much better than he did the rookies. Most likely, he felt the veterans had paid their dues. Van Brocklin had great respect for the game and felt it was an honor to have played in the NFL. He thought veteran players should teach the younger players and serve as role models.

Those who knew Van Brocklin often speak of his generosity. He loved children and showed them the other side of his powerful personality. His friends and players say he was "as nice a guy as you would ever want to meet" off the football field. But his personal on-the-field drive toward victory brought about the reputation he held as a real tough guy.

When the words "tough guy" are mentioned, it is hard to leave former 12-year cornerback of the Minnesota Vikings, Ed Sharockman, out of the conversation. No. 45 guarded the flank for the Purple from 1962 to 1972 in fine fashion at the old Metropolitan Stadium. He was a ferocious hitter and played with a marvelous passion.

Many professions have the luxury to easily correct any mistakes that have been made. Sometimes, a flaw or a bad decision may even go unnoticed. The public seldom learns and very rarely cares about the intricate details of most business occupations.

But one profession exists in which every mistake is a public confession. As an NFL cornerback, any blunder you make is seen by 50,000 people sitting right before you. The mistake is often reflected on a giant scoreboard and later, millions of fans hear about it on radio and television.

Therefore, if a friend complains of the stress they are facing on the job, it may be appropriate to ask, "Oh, do you play cornerback in the National Football League?" Drafted out of the University of Pittsburgh, Ed Sharockman did, and he played the position well for over a decade.

Ed is a fine person and real gentleman with deep religious convictions and a caring personality. He speaks very highly of Van Brocklin. "Van Brocklin was very intelligent and he knew the game. He set up a great offensive game plan and he had a big heart. If you were down and out, he was there to help you out," says Sharockman.

Sharockman recalls that, during his first year, he was injured and did not have enough cash to travel home. Van Brocklin loaned him the money and Ed never forgot it. He paid everything back, but the coach's gesture registered with Sharockman in his time of need and remains some 45 years later. "I remember another time when he gave money to a family where the husband and father had died," say Sharockman. The Dutchman was just that kind of person.

When former Baltimore Colt and Vikings player Don Joyce's career was near an end, Van Brocklin asked him whether he wanted to stay with the Vikings as a backup player or be traded to another team where he could play on a regular basis. He told Joyce he would do whatever the athlete wanted. He delivered on his word, and Joyce has never forgotten it.

After retirement, Joyce accepted a coaching position at De La Salle High School in Minneapolis, Minnesota. He recalls countless days between 1963 and 1967 in which Van Brocklin, uninvited, would turn up at practice to spend time with the high school football players. "It really meant a lot to those kids to have the

Minnesota Vikings head coach show up at their practice," says Joyce. Van Brocklin did so because he enjoyed it and felt it was important.

Longtime friend and traveling companion Shelley Walsh speaks of the Norm Van Brocklin he knew and what a great friend he was. They traveled together and associated with one another for many years. Walsh called The Dutchman a "wonderful father and great family man." Van Brocklin had three daughters, adopted three others, and always found time to interact with them all.

Walsh remembers many an afternoon in Edina, Minnesota, watching Van Brocklin toss a football around with the kids. Here was the former great Eagle quarterback, Minnesota Vikings head coach, and future Hall of Famer lofting passes to a bunch of youngsters on Walsh's front lawn.

Although Van Brocklin did not possess the same demeanor he held on Sundays in the fall as he played out in the yard, Shelley Walsh does recall a time on vacation when a game of darts in an Ireland pub brought out that fire in The Dutchman.

The patrons soon became amazed as dart after dart struck the bull's-eye. They wondered who this man was as the darts glazed by his ear on their way to the center of the target. The looks on their faces soon conveyed their thoughts: "This guy can throw those darts!"

Little did the patrons know they were watching one of the greatest passers in NFL history in the pub that afternoon. They never found who he was, and it didn't matter, as Van Brocklin ingratiated himself with the participants as well as interested bystanders through his skill.

Van Brocklin's on-field competitiveness and incredible desire for victory brought about a public image quite different from that seen by his family. "He was a very loving and gentle father who was sensitive and very sympathetic," says Kirby Vanderyt, one of Van Brocklin's daughters. "He stressed the importance of us getting an education and always being polite to others."

Very generous with his personal time, Van Brocklin attended and spoke at many banquets and found it very difficult to turn down those asking for his assistance. But once the former quarterback and driven head coach left the stadium, he was a gardener and baker. "He loved to bake bread and work in his garden," said Vanderyt, and, after a loss, "He found such things as raking leaves to help him escape from the defeat."

When the best of game plans fell to destruction and rubble, even the quiet, serene act of moving leaves around a yard helped Van Brocklin become a different person—the man loved by family and friends.

But he never really got away from the game. At dinner, it was not unusual for The Dutchman to begin drawing up plays on a napkin. His mind was always tuned into the game. Sometimes, he would wake in the middle of the night to draw up a new configuration for his next game.

Bill McGrane, the Vikings' public relations director during part of Van Brocklin's tenure, remembers sitting in the back of a duck boat with the coach on a Saturday morning, one day before the Vikings were scheduled to play the Packers. During the time of Green Bay "greatness" under Lombardi, it was predicted the Vikings would have little chance of staying in the game, let alone winning.

Suddenly, in the quiet of the early morning, Van Brocklin lost his attention to the duck-hunting task at hand, turned to McGrane, and said, "We're going to win tomorrow." McGrane looked back and replied, "Win? You mean against the Packers?"

That was precisely what he meant, and although McGrane doubted the proclamation would hold true, Van Brocklin was right.

The Vikings upset the Packers that Sunday, and as McGrane walked into the press conference, Van Brocklin looked across the room directly at him, nodded, and smiled. It was the resounding conclusion to their short conversation in the duck boat the day before. It was a very special smile and nod from a friend that will always be remembered.

Kirby Vanderyt describes her father as a man with a "strong personality and a big heart." She thoroughly enjoys speaking of her

Fran Tarkenton (No. 10) played quarterback for Minnesota during Van Brocklin's (left) reign as head coach of the Vikings. *Photo courtesy of the Minnesota Vikings*

father, saying, "He loved his family and was so proud to be an American. He was very secure in being who he was."

Along with gardening and baking, camping and family vacations became important parts of Van Brocklin's private life. He also enjoyed entertaining and had the team to his house on several occasions. "He had us greet the players by being polite and having a firm handshake," says Vanderyt, who was often in awe of the Viking players as they arrived. "I remember one party when I looked up the stairs and saw the shadow of this giant man walking in the hallway looking for the bathroom." She speaks with such passion as she describes the size of the lost visitor, and then proudly announces that it was the "great Carl Eller."

Former Viking Jim Lindsey describes Eller as the "greatest physical specimen I have ever seen." Says Lindsey, "It was as if he had been chiseled out of stone." One can only imagine how the great Purple giant looked to the little girl when she gazed up at the massive athlete as the Minnesota Vikings enjoyed their head coach's hospitality.

The eighth of nine children and the only to receive a college education, Van Brocklin was a proud man with great integrity. When the athlete was with the Eagles, the team doctor and friend died of a heart attack while painting his house. "Norm went out and finished the painting," says Bill McGrane.

Van Brocklin opened training camp in 1961 in Bemidji, Minnesota. Those who took part remember it as a "hitting"—an attempt to build a football team from the ground up to compete with the likes of the Packers and the Bears. But as the years went by, for some reason no championships were played, and the six seasons The Dutchman reigned as head coach of the Vikings were very tough times.

It wasn't a pleasant beginning, as Van Brocklin initially felt he was working with players who couldn't make it with other clubs and rookies who wouldn't make it with the Vikings. But as the early years evolved, so did a group of players who started at Bemidji, eventually becoming treasured household names. Mick Tingelhoff,

Jim Marshall, Carl Eller, Fred Cox, Fran Tarkenton, and so many others began to form the nucleus of a rich franchise history.

The Dutchman abruptly resigned in the spring of 1967. His time with the Vikings was over. In difficult and stormy times, Van Brocklin won only 29 games those first six years. The losses and ties, all 55 of them, were unacceptable. He was never able to bring his team to the threshold he had attained as a player. And then it was over.

Once Fran Tarkenton was traded to the New York Giants, the franchise faced the departure of its starting quarterback and head coach prior to the 1967 season. It didn't take long, however, to place the Vikings in capable hands, as one of our own returned to the frozen tundra of the Northland—though he actually came from Winnipeg, Manitoba. It didn't matter. Harry Peter "Bud" Grant was named head coach of the Minnesota Vikings.

And, as Bill McGrane so eloquently entitled his book, *BUD: The Other Side of the Glacier*, by Harper and Row Publishers in 1986, fans soon found out what Grant's appointment meant some 19 years before Mr. McGrane ever wrote about him.

Norm Van Brocklin went on to coach the Atlanta Falcons from October 1968 until 1974, when he was fired eight games into the season. The Dutchman had some good years in Atlanta and made the Falcons very competitive, but his tenure there also came to a sudden ending.

After leaving the coaching ranks for good, Van Brocklin retired to his home in the middle of a pecan farm in Social Circle, Georgia. As he told longtime friend Shelley Walsh about he and his wife's new residence, "We are the Dutch and the Dutchess of Social Circle."

# 3

# BUD GRANT

THE DETROIT LIONS had completed their pregame warm up and were making final preparations in their locker room. The kickoff of a nationally televised game between the Minnesota Vikings and the Detroit Lions was scheduled for noon in Pontiac, Michigan.

However, a problem existed. The Vikings had not completed their pregame warm up; in fact, they hadn't even begun. To make matters worse, they were not in the locker room, nor anyplace to be found. The game was approaching start time, and the reality was, THE VIKINGS WERE NOT AT THE STADIUM!

NFL executives, television network personnel, and other individuals with any game coordination responsibilities were in a full-fledged panic. All finite planning and attention to detail had collapsed into a state of total confusion. No NFL game had ever neared kickoff time with only one team on the field.

Fans seated in the stadium and those watching the broadcast probably wouldn't have appreciated it had the decision-makers started the game on time with some sort of Lions intra-squad scrimmage. So they waited.

The Vikings were to be some 40 minutes late, as they were stranded on a freeway in a horrendous traffic jam, resulting in some of the Lion faithful to believe, "This is the doing of Bud Grant!"

Under Grant, the Vikings had held the Lions at bay for years, winning games in extraordinary ways. The numerous victories resulted in an incredible winning record against their division rivals. The assumption of some that Grant had devised the "infamous freeway game plan" was never proven. But we'll let you decide.

Harry Peter "Bud" Grant became the leader of the Purple in 1967. Over the next four decades, the Vikings' head coach became the face of the franchise and a legend in the eyes of the Minnesota sporting public. Had there not been several years between his stardom status as a three-sport letterman at the University of Minnesota and his return to the state to coach the Vikings, his time as an icon would be even longer.

But it was not his great prowess as an athlete or his prolific success as a professional football coach that made him unique; it was more due to the fact that no one could really figure him out. He acted differently from others. He never looked sad or, in fact, happy. Fans couldn't tell from his actions how he felt after a last-second win or a devastating loss, and that confused and distanced them from him. He never seemed to smile, which further led to the mystique that surrounded him.

Norb Berg, one of the head coach's closest friends, has a favorite Grant "one-liner" that took place on national television. Phyllis George, famed television star and past *NFL Today* studio broadcaster, said to him during an interview before a game, "Smile, Bud." His reply was, "Say something funny, Phyllis"—a typical Grant response that listeners enjoyed.

Bud Grant press conferences and individual interviews were classics. He always had the upper hand, almost as if he had rehearsed. Was it in his nature to allow such long silences before he answered a question? Was he thinking carefully about the response, or did he genuinely thrive on watching reporters squirm? No one knew for sure, but either way, his pauses were renowned.

If the media interviews demonstrated one way Grant was unlike his followers, then his coaching demeanor really perplexed them. Watching him on the sidelines during a football game was a unique

Harry Peter "Bud" Grant began his long tenure with the Minnesota Vikings when named head coach in 1967. *Photo courtesy of the Minnesota Vikings*

experience. Had the background noise, headphones, sweatshirt, and hat been removed, no one would have known for sure what he was doing or the nature of his profession. An NFL football coach on a Sunday afternoon? Hardly. But he was—and a great one, at that.

"Only one time in all the years I worked with Bud did I ever see any emotion come from him because of a win or a loss," says Mike Lynn, former executive and general manager of the Vikings for 17 years. "It was after the Dallas loss in the playoffs in 1975."

It will be difficult for Viking faithful to read this, because the bad memory of that game never seems to fade away. The Vikings had perhaps their greatest team ever in 1975 and had all but won against the Cowboys with seconds to play.

It was the infamous Hail Mary pass from Roger Staubach to Drew Pearson in a waning fourth period that knocked the Vikings out of the playoffs and another trip to the Super Bowl. But it wasn't just the catch in the game's closing moments, it was the fact that Pearson pushed off Vikings defensive back Nate Wright without being handed a penalty that hurt the most.

A devastating defeat, it remains a horrifying memory even some 30 years later. But at the time, the enormity of the loss was much more difficult for someone as close to it as the head coach. Lynn came to the office the following day and spoke briefly to Grant. The loss was hard enough for Lynn to accept, and he was very troubled by it. But Grant's response to the defeat was what bothered Lynn the most. In all the years they had worked together, Lynn had never seen the coach so down.

"Bud was very down after that loss, and it was the only time I ever saw him that way," said Lynn. "It shook me up so much to see him like that. I called my wife and told her, 'We're out of here. We are leaving.' I was going to quit, just because of the reaction of Bud."

With great passion, Lynn describes Grant as a "wonderful coach." Lynn has a high regard for Bud and they had a great relationship. "He was so steady," said Lynn, "and it didn't matter if they won or lost. He was always the same." Except for that one time.

The fans had an incredible identification with Grant and the Purple. The Vikings' connection to the area has been like a beautiful marriage. The community has embraced the Vikings and the relationship has lasted. Grant was a strong believer that the team "owed something to the fans." The team needed to be as loyal to the fans as the fans were to the team. Grant believed the team needed to "give back" to the fans to show appreciation for their loyalty.

The old Metropolitan Stadium hosted the great relationship between fans and players as they held conversations in the parking lot before home games and tailgated together afterward. Grant wanted and expected his players to take part in each event, and the fans loved it. It was Bud's way, and he felt it was very important.

There is something exceptional about a person who is easily recognized by his first name. Mickey? Mickey Mantle, of course. Willie? Why, that has to be the great Willie Mays. And Elvis? Enough said. In Minnesota, "Bud" is all that needs to be said for every sports fan—and even many others—to know the conversation must be about Bud Grant.

Many Viking followers have kept Grant in their own very personal place reserved for legends. Without ever knowing or even meeting him, strong opinions and descriptions of Grant have been shaped by fans through memories of his leadership with the beloved Purple.

Viking fan and proud loyalist Frank Wood gives his view of Grant. "As a longtime Viking fan, I always admired Bud Grant's solemn, no-nonsense approach to coaching," says Wood, who respects and admires the head coach for his accomplishments and just for being Bud. "He was a confident and courageous leader who held himself and his players to the highest standards of integrity and performance on and off the field. He motivated his players, coaches, and the fans. HE IS THE GREATEST!"

Although the public rarely saw any of his emotions during even the most dramatic moments of a professional football game, there was another side to Grant. "He was the greatest practical joker of all time," said former Vikings quarterback Bob Lee, who played for Grant for nine seasons.

Lee recalled a time when the team traveled to Tulsa for practice during one of their successful playoff runs, which kept the team out of town over the Christmas holidays. The players had agreed to draw names and give Christmas presents to each other. The plan was that each gift would be received without a card, so the sender would remain unidentified.

At the time, three quarterbacks were listed on the Vikings roster, and they all had common backgrounds. Fran Tarkenton, Bob Berry, and Lee had, at one time in their careers, played for Norm Van Brocklin. During their times together, each had experienced highs and lows with the great quarterback and Hall of Famer.

When the presents were opened, the three Viking quarterbacks found that they had each received an identical coffee mug. On the outside of the mug was a picture holder. Each mug contained a photo of Van Brocklin with an inscription reading, "All is forgiven, Norm."

They all knew Grant had done it, but could never pick up the slightest of clues to be absolutely sure. He just stood in the back of the room and took it all in. The prank was vintage Bud Grant.

Jerry Burns, offensive coordinator for the Vikings under Grant for 17 years and head coach of the team from 1986 to 1991, had the reputation of being afraid of almost any type of bug, reptile, or anything small that moved. It was not an unusual occurrence for Jerry to open up a projector and see something crawl or fly out of it.

Doug Sutherland, one of the great Viking linemen who played next to Carl Eller, Jim Marshall, and Alan Page for many years, loves Bud's sense of humor and ability to pull off a practical joke without taking any responsibility for it.

Sutherland remembers Burns once began a film session by jumping over two rows of chairs and almost killing himself to avoid a butterfly that had escaped from the movie projector. Apparently, Grant's signature was also on top of an occasional snake left in one of Burns' desk drawers. The head coach's name was written all over each of the pranks, but no one really knew for sure.

Bud Grant brought to the Vikings an incredible reputation as a great athlete at the University of Minnesota. Grant earned four letters in football, three in basketball, and two in baseball from 1946 to

1949. He followed this with a stint with the great Minneapolis Lakers basketball team and the Philadelphia Eagles football team, and then disappeared across the Canadian border to play for the Winnipeg Blue Bombers.

Grant stayed with the Blue Bombers for several years and, after participating in six Grey Cup Championship games, took over as head coach at the age of 29. His leadership qualities led him to coaching several years before he was really ready to retire as a player, and Bud felt to continue at both positions would not fare well in the long run. So he retired from playing and led the Blue Bombers to four Grey Cup Championships as their head coach.

The Vikings had given some consideration to Grant as their first head coach when the team arrived in the Twin Cities, but the timing wasn't right. However, when 1967 came and the Vikings had parted ways with The Dutchman, Bud Grant was the perfect fit. He stayed until 1983 and then returned again for the 1985 season to bring credibility and order back to the franchise after a devastating 1984 season.

During his span with the Vikings, Grant won 168 games, lost 108, and tied five. Minnesota won 11 division titles under Grant, made the playoffs 12 times, and played in four Super Bowls.

Grant was a Pro Bowl player with the Eagles and is a member of the Canadian League Football Hall of Fame and the National Football League Hall of Fame, being voted in in 1983 and 1994, respectfully.

With all his accomplishments in the collegiate and professional ranks, one would think the records are what stand out in Grant's life, and they probably do hold some significance; however, his family is undeniably most important to him.

Grant seems most satisfied when he proudly proclaims, "I have six children that all graduated from college and 19 grandchildren, and they all live within 30 minutes of Winter Park," the Vikings' headquarters. The momentous athletic feats, the Hall of Fame coaching records, the trips to the Super Bowl, and the revered status he has acclaimed are all a distant second to his role as a husband, father, and grandfather.

He has an incredible outlook on life. After being associated with the Minnesota Vikings franchise for 40 years as the coach and face of the organization, when asked to describe what it has all meant to him, he again puts everything in the right perspective. "It was a living," says Grant. "It put food on the table for my family. I wasn't a brain surgeon or an airline pilot. I was in the entertainment business."

Grant describes being coach of the Vikings as a job he liked to do. He didn't want a vagabond lifestyle and thrived on being in the same place for an extended period of time.

Bud grew up during the Depression, and times were tough. He recalls walking in the street as opposed to sidewalks because he had a better chance to find loose change there. His dad was a firefighter and the family didn't have a lot of money.

"I remember being hungry all the time," Grant says. However, he is quick to point out that countless other families were in the same situation during those difficult times. Grant wanted to make sure that no one felt sorry for him as a youngster. With his background and level perspective, it all makes sense. Coaching was a living. The pluses came because he liked it and was very good at it.

As the head coach of the Minnesota Vikings, he won and he won often. But the enigma of his character always seemed to attract the most attention. It was perhaps what identified him the most among the players who knew him well and the fans who thought they did. He had developed a sort of peaceful assurance that everything was going to be all right no matter what the situation.

Longtime friend and Viking colleague Fred Zamberletti emphasizes that faith by describing what many players have told him throughout the years. "If they were lost in the woods and had to find one person to get them out of there, it would be Bud Grant," he says. "It was because of his leadership."

Zamberletti knows Bud Grant well. When Zamberletti was employed at Iowa early in his career, he remembers a young, athletic basketball player traveling with the University of Minnesota team to Iowa City for a game. "There was something that just stood out about this young man," recalls Fred. He had no idea at the time that

The ferocious Bill Brown (No. 30) leaps over opponents and teammates alike as he pursues the end zone. *Photo courtesy of the Minnesota Vikings*

their careers would come together and Bud Grant would become his boss, friend, and colleague for over 40 years.

Employees and players alike never wanted to disappoint Bud Grant. He instilled an incredible loyalty among these great athletes and colleagues and treated them well. He was a "master at his work" and maintained a calmness and confidence that was contagious. It was a cornerstone of his success.

Fred Cox recalls a game when the Vikings were behind 17-0, and yet there was never a doubt in the kicker's mind that they would prevail at the end. And they did. Grant's make-up inspired a confidence in his players that, if they believed in him and did things his way, they had a chance to be successful. A "chance" may have been the belief sold to them; however, "would be successful" may have been the better way to put it.

He was deeply loyal to players who had reciprocated that loyalty for many years. He would often keep players "one more year" to better prepare them for their lives outside of football as they neared retirement age. Bill Brown is a great example of that.

There may never have been a tougher player to wear the Purple than Bill Brown. He came out of Illinois to the Chicago Bears and was traded to the Vikings. No. 30 played at Minnesota for 13 years. He ran with the football harder than most and liked to hit people. It was his trademark and at the top of his resume.

Jerry Burns coached with the great Vince Lombardi at Green Bay before joining the Vikings in 1968. He says Lombardi used to mention only a couple of players who had the ability to totally upset what the Packers planned to do on a given Sunday. One of those players was Bill Brown.

Brown carried the ball and abused his body and others for Grant from 1967 until he retired in 1974. Grant appreciated Brown, his work ethic, and his loyalty. He made the athlete captain of special teams his last year, and Brown delivered in the role the way Bud knew he would. It was a tribute to the great Viking player.

Grant was always in charge and left little doubt, even in the most unsettling of circumstances, such as the Detroit game referenced earlier. Even the most sturdy of leaders might have come unraveled had his football team been 40 minutes late for a nationally televised game.

The day got off to a rough start. The Vikings were on the way to the stadium in Pontiac, Michigan, to play the Lions. Grant always wanted to arrive one hour and 10 minutes before a game was scheduled to start. He strongly believed that players would waste energy sitting around the locker room ruminating about the game.

He had experienced this often during his playing career and kept it from the routine as the head coach.

Arrive at the game with little time to dress, get out on the field for the pregame warm-up, get back to the locker room for final preparations, and go play the game. It was a successful approach and had worked well for many years. Grant's typical agenda didn't factor into this game, however.

The Vikings' plans went amiss as their buses were stuck in a horrendous traffic jam on the freeway leading to Pontiac. The national network folks were in a fury and the NFL executives buzzed as well. The game was ready to start, so WHERE WERE THE VIKINGS?

Stu Voigt, the steady-handed, great blocking tight end under Grant, speaks of the situation on the way into the stadium, actually finding some humor in it all. Voigt says the Vikings' bus driver was shaken by what was occurring and, as he maneuvered the bus into the parking lot, he hollered out the window at a parking attendant for assistance. "I GOT THE VIKINGS! I GOT THE VIKINGS!" he bellowed out the window, hoping for some clearance to approach the stadium. The parking lot attendant nearby provided little accommodation as he hollered back, "I GOT THE LIONS AND FIVE POINTS!"

When the Vikings finally entered the locker room, everyone was rushing to get onto the field. Fred Zamberletti, Viking trainer at the time, happened to be standing next to Grant when referee Bob Frederich approached the coach like a Prussian general in a state of rage.

"The league is going to fine you for this and I am penalizing you 15 yards on the opening kickoff," said Frederich. Fire exuded from his mouth and anger coursed through his body as Bud looked at him and asked, "Is there anything else that we can help you with today?"

Showing little emotion from the surrounding chaos, the man in charge then turned to his hurried players and prepped them on how to handle the situation. "Take your time. They can't play the game without you," said Bud.

And when it was over, the long record of Lion futility against Grant's Vikings continued, as the late-arriving Purple won 10-9 on a blocked kick. Some have said the Vikings really won the game while stalled on the freeway.

The following year's trip to Detroit was very different. Jeff Diamond, who had come to the Vikings right out of college as a journalism and political science major at the University of Minnesota, had been assigned to take care of the team's travel arrangements. Initially hired as an intern to work on various projects, including a book on the first 15 years of the franchise, Diamond would stay with the team for the next 23 years and become a major part of the team's front office and Vikings history.

Obviously, the trip to Pontiac was of major importance. Diamond was not about to deal with the horrendous nightmare they had the previous year. He planned the team's arrival at the stadium to the most intricate detail. He hired a police escort, talked to numerous people who knew the area and its traffic patterns, and found the most direct route by back roads that would have little congestion. And he allowed a full 45 minutes for the trip, still staying within Grant's guidelines of arrival one hour and 10 minutes before kickoff.

Diamond's planning was masterful. In fact, the particulars were so well thought out that the team arrived in 20 minutes, significantly earlier than planned. This presented another problem.

As the head coach got off the bus, he looked at Diamond in that Bud Grant stare symbolic of his nature when things weren't going well, and said, "We're awfully early." Diamond had the words all scripted for his response, which would have eloquently stated something to the effect of, "Well, it's better than last year." Wisdom prevailed, however, and Diamond replied, "Bud, we'll get it right next time."

It was Jeff Diamond's second trip to Pontiac. In his first year with the team, he was on one of the busses stuck in traffic, but didn't have to worry because he was not yet in charge of travel. In fact, he fondly remembers parts of that first trip's account. Maybe it was Fran Tarkenton running up and down the aisle of the bus announcing that he was "doing his pregame warm-ups" that lightened the mood, or maybe it was just realizing he was a part of history that made it all so interesting. In any event, little did he know that next year he would be the one directing them to Pontiac to play the Detroit Lions.

Grant was always in charge and showed little emotion when handling responsibility, and the Minnesota Vikings represented that ideal on the field. The fans always seemed to know everything was under control. Even a hyped-up player from time to time tried to challenge Bud's decision-making during a game—it just never worked.

Bud never allowed anyone to take the upper hand in a situation. He simply had the last word and sometimes said very little to get it. His authority was never in doubt.

Fred Cox says he always stood right next to Grant on the sidelines whenever the Vikings neared the 50-yard line, ready for a field goal try if the course of action so dictated. "I never wanted Grant to have to look for me," says Cox.

Cox says that once, Bud ordered a player off the field for committing a penalty at a key time in the game. The player was outraged and ran at Grant to tell him of his dismay, obviously preparing to get in Grant's face and scream something like, "DON'T YOU EVER TAKE ME OUT OF A GAME LIKE THAT AGAIN!" Grant quickly looked the player in the eye, calmly said, "Go sit down," and directed his attention back to the game. "It was over," said Cox. "Done. Nothing else to be said."

Occasionally, players tried to usurp Bud's authority regarding the Vikings' practice schedule or other team rules and procedures. Bud made it reasonably comfortable for players to speak with him if they had an issue or concern. Sometimes, they would take it too far. It wasn't unusual for Bud to respond to an unreasonable request with, "We do it this way because I'm the guy with the whistle."

Speaking of whistles, Bud always blew his to end practice. Everyone knew that practice was over when the whistle blew, and it became a routine anticipated by the players.

Bob Lurtsema, great character and face of "THE OLD BENCHWARMER" status, once stole Bud's whistle during practice, and everyone waited to see how Bud would end practice that day. "He didn't even reach for the whistle," said Lurtsema. "He just said, 'Practice is over,' and left. He spoiled the whole thing!"

An avid outdoorsman, Grant spends a major part of his recreational time fishing and hunting. During hunting season in the fall, the Vikings always practiced early on days before home games. Grant would bring his hunting dogs to Saturday morning practices and tie them to a fence. As soon as practice ended, he would retrieve the dogs to go hunting.

One Saturday, a player approached Bud and asked, "Bud, how come we have to practice early Saturday morning so you can go hunting the rest of the day, and yet you won't let us go hunting?" Bud looked at him, replied, "Because I'm not playing tomorrow," and walked away. End of discussion.

As Grant's character unfolded, it was obvious to his players that he would not tolerate mental errors. They were unacceptable. Doug Sutherland called Grant "The General." "He treated you like a man," says Sutherland. "He understood the game and would not put up with missed assignments, late hits, and mental mistakes."

"Bud would not tolerate a player making one mistake. There were 22 starting players on a football team, and allowing that would mean 22 mistakes. He would not accept it," Sutherland says. "A game may be decided by one touchdown or less, so mistakes could not be allowed."

Jeff Siemon, great middle linebacker for the Vikings from 1972 to 1982, recalls Grant saying, "We can't do anything about players' speed, their size, or their strength, but we can do something about their mental mistakes."

The head coach liked intelligent players and players who stayed on the field, not in the training room. When he was speaking of the 40-year Viking anniversary team, he says, "If there was one ingredient that made this group successful, it was their durability." Toughness and greatness are often common denominators in Grant's way of thinking.

At times, a mistake, incident, or player's behavior would rankle Grant; however, his handling of such an episode was legendary. He never went out of his way to embarrass a player, but would find a way to make a subtle point.

One evening, the Vikings were being served a pregame meal in a beautiful ballroom at an Atlanta hotel. The meal's typical entrée was steak. On this particular night, Carl Eller, All-America Minnesota Gopher, Viking Hall of Famer, and legendary Purple People Eater, politely asked one of the waiters for pancakes in place of the customary steak dinner. The waiter told him it would be fine and he would shortly bring him the pancakes.

A few minutes went by, and no pancakes arrived. When Eller saw the waiter nearby, he again asked for the pancakes, and was told they were on the way. Still no pancakes were brought to Eller. Eller asked for the pancakes a third time and was told by the waiter that the coach had informed him that everyone would be eating steak for the pregame meal.

Eller flew into a rage, jumped up from his chair, and kicked a tray of steaks sitting nearby high into the air. Everyone in the room kept one eye on the plates, steaks, and other parts of the meal flying all around them, but left the other on Grant to see what his reaction would be.

The head coach looked up from his plate to see the steaks, plates, and food flying around the ballroom, looked back down at his plate, finished his meal, and left. No one could believe it. He had said nothing and seemed undisturbed by what had just occurred.

The Vikings' next pregame meal was somewhat different. There were no steaks. Each player was served two pancakes, each the size of a silver dollar. Grant never said anything, but his unspoken words filled the room: "You want pancakes? Here are your pancakes." The message was received and no more would be said. That was Bud Grant.

Sometimes players felt it necessary to send subtle messages of their own to Grant. It rarely, if ever, worked. Somehow, when their valiant attempts to gain the upper hand were carefully put into place and seemingly foolproof, in the end, Grant still prevailed.

One plan had all the makings of perfection. Every player was involved, with the goal to send a very distinct message to the head coach in "uniform" fashion. Bud Grant was an absolute stickler on every player dressing exactly the same. He didn't want anything on the uniform to stand out and felt strongly that the Vikings were a "team." They all needed to look the same; no individual would be set apart because of the way he was dressed.

The uniforms included long, royal blue socks that fit under the football pants at the knee. Over those socks were white socks, which rose about to the center point between the ankle and middle of the shin. Some players liked to pull the white socks up higher, stretch them to the knee, and then tape them up.

This was very unsettling to Grant. The socks were out of order and the tape stood out. These players looked different from the others, and he was not going to have it. So Grant instructed "Stubby" Eason, longtime Viking equipment manager, to buy clear tape so it would not be seen, and then asked him to order short white socks that could not be stretched. Because the tape was invisible, the players could still tape up their socks, but the socks would all be the same length—no exceptions.

The players thought Grant's action to control every aspect of their apparel overkill and exceeded his authority, so they decided to send him a message. Before football practice one morning at training camp in Mankato, Minnesota, every player went out on the field wearing "Bud's order," brand-new white socks. However, they weren't pulled up, but rolled in the other direction—downward, around the ankles. The last laugh would surely be on the coach: "You want our socks to be uniform? Well, here they are! Our socks are now uniform!"

Bud was always the last person to arrive on the practice field, so the players were all waiting to see how he would react. Showing up Bud Grant was big. It was going to be quite an experience and one to remember. This time they had him, and there was no escape.

Grant came out of the locker room, across the street, and through the large gate to the practice area. Awaiting his arrival on the field was a group of gifted athletes dressed in purple, socks rolled down around their ankles. The coach walked onto the practice field and started practice. Grant's socks were also rolled down around his ankles.

The Purple faithful always knew they were in capable hands with Grant in charge.

Mick Tingelhoff, a magnificent Vikings center for 17 years, said, "Many people who knew him feel the way they do about life because of Bud Grant. He was more than football to many of us. He lived a clean life and set a good example for us. He was the best example of the best man I ever met. He never swore, he never smoked, and he never got drunk. He was just a regular guy."

Other coaches might have had the Xs and Os of the game figured out better than Grant. They might have been able to walk up to a black board and diagram plays and defenses better, but few understood people better. He knew coaching and leadership included more than just internal aspects of the game. He understood that character and the ability to handle others is critical to success.

Stu Voigt says that Grant was the first coach to really understand the concept of a "team game." He made kicking and punting as important as anything else, which paid off as the Vikings won many times on great kicking, punting, and blocking kicks.

"He looked for the 'good guys' to be on his team and for the ones who could 'make the plays,'" states Voigt. Grant commented many times that "he never cut anyone from the team, they cut themselves. Make the plays, and be one of the good guys." It was a simple formula.

Fred Cox played for Grant from 1967 until 1977. Standing beside the head coach throughout so many games taught him a great deal about a man that truly knew people. "He was the epitome of a man who knew how to handle others," says Cox. "He was a great judge of character."

Cox remembers playing the last game of one season in Detroit. He missed three field goals in the game and sat before his locker afterward, devastated by his performance. Thoughts about the long off-season and what his future might be with the team were very difficult for the kicker to endure.

Bud walked up to Cox, put his arm around him, and said, "Bet you never had a game like that before." The calm and supportive manner in which he spoke said that, as Cox puts it, "He understood that I had a lousy game, but it didn't mean that I wasn't going to be with the team next year."

What Bud did for him that afternoon in Detroit meant a great deal to Fred Cox. That was Bud Grant.

Grant was also genuinely concerned about people. Cox's first wife had some very difficult years and had been in and out of the hospital often during his career with the Vikings. One day, he was called into Grant's office and asked if his playing football had anything to do with his wife's illness. Fred told Bud he didn't believe there was a connection.

Cox feels that, if there had been, Bud would have released him from the team. Family was more important than football. Grant's passion throughout their conversation that day will always remain with the kicker.

Bud Grant was special. Maybe the greatest of players weren't around during the head coach's career, but the Vikings won and they believed in him. And Grant believed in them.

Often on a fourth down in crucial situations, Grant would look over at Cox and ask, "What do you think?" Near the end of his career, the 39-year-old managed a 52-yard field goal. Grant had asked Cox if he thought he could make the kick. Cox told him "yes" and delivered.

The face of the Minnesota Vikings and a part of our lives for over 40 years, Bud Grant continues on with his life in his way. He keeps an office at Winter Park, and frequents it often. He still takes an endless pause before answering questions, but always provides wisdom and common sense in his answers. Bob Lee is right when he says, "When you walk out of an office after a meeting with Bud Grant, you just feel better."

He does that to you, maybe because he has accomplished so much in his life, or maybe because he's Bud Grant—that's just who he is. Whatever the reason, that feeling is special. He is special.

And you know what else? In front of all those cameras and millions of viewers on the *NFL Today* show, I think Bud would have smiled had Phyllis said something funny.

# 4

# THE FRONT
# OFFICE

TRAVELING WITH THE MINNESOTA VIKINGS football team, Bill McGrane was uncomfortable throughout the flight. He was sitting in the coach section near the rear of the plane. The sounds, air turbulence, and bumpy ride were making him very uneasy. Calmly reading a magazine next to him was Vikings general manager Jim Finks.

Distressed by the circumstances, McGrane looked over at Finks and said, "Jim, why do we always have to sit in the same seats in the back of the plane, close to the engine? The noise and rough ride are terrible!" Finks looked up over his glasses at McGrane and replied, "When is the last time you heard about one of these #%#@#%%# back into a mountain?"

McGrane put up with the general manager's seat location preference on this particular flight and many others with the Vikings and later, the Chicago Bears. Very simply put, it was where Jim Finks felt comfortable.

"He was the most unforgettable person I have ever met," says Bill McGrane. "He had so many positive qualities. He was a great evaluator of people, a great leader, had a wonderful sense of humor, and was very bright."

McGrane speaks about Finks with deep passion and great loyalty. "Jim just happened to be in football. He could have been a leader in

Washington, the president of a college, or a general in the military. He was very gifted," recalls McGrane.

McGrane and Finks worked together with the Vikings from 1966 to 1972. Bill left for the league office for a couple years and then joined Finks with the Chicago Bears in the mid-'70s. He truly enjoyed his friend, who had been a great player, a great leader, and an outstanding person.

Like many others, Bill McGrane speaks of Jim Finks in a positive manner, reflecting great honor and respect. When someone makes a noteworthy comment about Finks during a conversation, others reverently reply, "That was Jim."

Finks was known as a tough negotiator, but fair to most. Former Viking and one of the great faces of the franchise, Jim Marshall speaks of Jim Finks with the highest of regard.

"Jim Finks will always be one of the nicest, fairest, kindest people I have ever met," says Marshall. "He was one of the best general managers in sports and had a real caring for players."

Marshall did some work as a player representative for the team during his playing years in the '60s, and says that Finks was always welcome at player meetings because the players respected him. This unusual occurrence was indicative of who he was and how players felt about the general manager.

Before Finks joined the Vikings, Norm Van Brocklin had become the power and authority of the franchise. Once Bert Rose and Joe Thomas left the organization, the front office role and general management of the Vikings became Finks' responsibility. And he got along well with The Dutchman, as each understood the other's duties and responsibilities.

It likely was a good relationship because Finks wasn't just another hire. He wasn't simply another administrator, and he

---

Jim Finks, one-time legendary general manager of the Minnesota Vikings, was inducted into the Pro Football Hall of Fame in 1995.
*Photo courtesy of the Minnesota Vikings*

certainly wasn't front-office window dressing. Now a Hall of Famer, Jim Finks' track record speaks for itself.

If one were to look up information from the Pro Football Hall of Fame in Canton, Ohio, a listing would be found that summarizes his dedication, commitment, and expertise in the profession of football. It would read:

"THE PRO FOOTBALL HALL OF FAME—CANTON, OHIO

JIM FINKS—CLASS OF '95—ADMINISTRATOR"

The above is quite brief, yet a lasting and thorough evaluation of Jim Finks' career in professional football. It sums everything all up. Jim Finks was recognized for his achievements and recognized for his abilities. He was something very special.

Finks was brought in from the Canadian Football League to run the Minnesota Vikings' front office in 1964. He had conquered some early leadership squabbles among the owners with respect to who would fill the role of general manager and run the Vikings.

After a meeting with all of the team owners, subsequent to part owner Ole Haugsrud initiating contact, the vote became unanimous that Jim Finks would take control of the franchise's daily activities.

With Van Brocklin also sold on the idea, it was clear that Finks was the right choice.

The two had competed against each other during their illustrious careers and had great respect for one another's football prowess on and off the field. Once assured by The Dutchman that he had no interest in leading both on and off the field, Finks was ready to leave Calgary and become the general manager of the Minnesota Vikings. It was one of the great decisions in franchise history.

Jim Finks' background is legendary. He was a great athlete, an incredible administrator, and a marvelous judge of player talent. Unfortunately and very sadly, he died just a year before he was elected to the Pro Football Hall of Fame. Lung cancer took his life in 1994 at the age of 66.

The Vikings' general manager was born in St. Louis, Missouri, on August 31, 1927, a historic year in professional sports. Not only was

Finks, one of the greatest administrators in pro football, born, but Babe Ruth also hit 60 home runs that year.

Finks became an administrator with a reputation of such honor, expertise, and distinction that it earned him election into the Pro Football Hall of Fame in 1995, in Canton, Ohio. It was the ultimate in recognition for his years of football greatness.

In his eulogy at Jim Finks' funeral, Ed McCaskey, Chairman of the Board of the Chicago Bears, was quoted saying, "I know most of the NFL owners rather well. Some are fine men, capable men, rich men, and some are lucky men. But for one reason or another, they all have achieved membership in what has proven to be a very exclusive club. Jim Finks stood head and shoulders above them all—in all areas."

How does a man become honored in such a way? To be worthy of such adoration, his lifetime must have been filled with achievement, expertise, integrity, and credibility. And it was. With Jim Finks, you got the whole package.

Finks attended the University of Tulsa and was drafted by the Pittsburgh Steelers in the 12th round of the NFL Draft in 1949. He played in Pittsburgh as a defensive back and quarterback for several years before retiring at the end of the 1955 season.

Keeping the great Johnny Unitas on the bench while starting as the Steelers' quarterback became one of Finks' major claims to fame. Unitas, who was drafted by Pittsburgh in 1955, was later cut the same year and eventually went to the Baltimore Colts, where the soon to be recognized Johnny U. became one of the greatest quarterbacks of all time.

That statement alone must be thought about a bit more thoroughly. Imagine that the main competition for your job is cut, fired, or dismissed, only to go on to greatness and prolific fame.

Jim Finks kept the job Johnny Unitas wanted. On the surface, this may not appear overly significant, until one sees the following facts regarding Unitas' career with the Baltimore Colts from *Pro Football Hall of Fame Records*:

"40,239 total yards passing, 290 touchdown passes thrown, 47 consecutive games throwing a touchdown pass, three times voted player of the year in the National Football League and named to the Pro Bowl 10 times."

And the Steelers let Unitas go for Finks. One would have to assume Finks was a pretty good quarterback during his Steelers playing days.

In 1956, Finks worked as an assistant coach under Terry Brennen at Notre Dame. The following year he went to Canada, where he stayed until 1964, serving as a player, assistant coach, scout, and eventually the general manager of the Calgary Stampeders.

It was in this locale that he came in contact with Bud Grant of the Winnipeg Blue Bombers. This relationship would eventually lead to their joining forces with the Minnesota Vikings in 1967.

Finks is highly regarded by most who knew him. Fred Zamberletti, iconic Vikings trainer and mentor in the organization for over four and a half decades, says when Finks arrived with the Vikings from Canada, he came in "almost as a guest."

He never exercised his authority, but got to know the organization and everyone in it. His style, his professionalism, and his wisdom were much loved by his colleagues, constituents, and subordinates.

When Finks came to the Vikings, Zamberletti says he had it all. "He had been a player, a coach, and had also been a general manager in Canada," Zamberletti explains. "He was well accepted through his reputation and mostly by the way he treated people."

Such treatment, however, takes nothing away from his ability as a tough negotiator. Zamberletti recalls a story involving Finks and former Vikings running back, Dave Osborn.

At that time in professional football history, agents had not yet arrived on the scene to represent players in contract negotiations with management. When it was time to negotiate his contract with Finks, Osborn decided to take some advice from Zamberletti.

Zamberletti and Osborn had been traveling together on a Vikings public relations tour. One night they began discussing

Osborn's contract for the next year. Says Zamberletti, "I told Ozzie to go into Finks' office and give him a blank contract and tell him, 'I have a lot of respect for you and I trust you, and I know you will be fair with me.'"

Osborn followed Zamberletti's guidance, handed Finks the blank contract, and left his office. He was elated when he found out that Finks had given the athlete the best contract he had ever received. The Vikings trainer had given the Vikings running back some pretty good financial counseling, paying out wonderful dividends.

At contract time the next year, Osborn was coming off a rather unproductive season. When he arrived at Finks' office, the manager told him, "Go back and tell Zamberletti it's going to be different this year!" Neither Osborn nor his "financial advisor" ever learned how Finks had found out.

Zamberletti, who had a deep affection for Finks, tells the story with a smile. Another time, Finks called Zamberletti to ask him about a particular player who had been injured. The player came to the Vikings from Atlanta and had not played at all when he broke his ankle in a non-related football injury.

Finks wanted to know the cost of the player's medical bills. "He paid for it and didn't want anyone else to know about it. He was that kind of a person—a real classy guy," says Zamberletti.

The year 1967 was a significant one in Minnesota Vikings history. Finks had traded Fran Tarkenton to the New York Giants and Norm Van Brocklin had resigned. It was time to bring in a new head coach and look for a new starting quarterback. The Minnesota Vikings organization faced some big decisions.

When Bert Rose brought the name "Vikings," which he felt represented the fiercest of competitors, to the owners, he also brought the color purple, which he fondly associated with the University of Washington. The Vikings and the Purple, name and color, were beginning the seventh year of an area love affair. The franchise was about to embark on an even greater effort in a manner unfamiliar to the Purple faithful—winning on Sunday afternoons—

with two great pro football leaders, Finks and Bud Grant, at the helm.

Finks went to Canada to bring in the Vikings' new head coach. Soon, Harry Peter "Bud" Grant arrived to take charge of the Purple and begin a dynasty.

The 1967 season was the beginning of a glory period in Vikings history that would deliver 11 divisional championships and four Super Bowl appearances over the next 14 years. Finks and Grant both knew how to win and be successful, and now they were doing it together.

Finks was instrumental in putting together winning teams through quality player trades and the NFL Draft. He ran the front office and Bud Grant delivered the work in final form—and deliver he did. They were quite the combination.

Trading Tarkenton to the Giants brought Finks players and draft choices, and his crafty move to return Tarkenton to the Vikings five years later in 1972 strengthened the franchise for most of the '70s.

Before Tarkenton's return, however, Finks conspired with Grant to bring Joe Kapp from the Canadian Football League to the Vikings. Both had become familiar with him through their experiences in Canada, and when it was time for the Vikings to find a new quarterback to lead the Purple, both knew Kapp was the player. Kapp remains in the hearts of the Vikings faithful some decades later, even though his time with the franchise lasted only a few years.

Finks' relationship with Grant in Canada had solidified his belief that the coach knew how to win and was the right person for the Vikings. Finks once told Bill McGrane that "it is very difficult to win in pro football and there are very few who can live with winning." He said Grant knew how to win and how to handle it. He further told McGrane that Grant was one of the few people he had met who was "comfortable with himself."

Regarding the hiring of Bud Grant, Finks was quoted saying, "I saw Bud in good times and bad times in Winnipeg while I was in Calgary. I know him as a man who knows how to win and how to retain his composure when he loses. And he isn't exactly obscure around here. He was an outstanding athlete at Minnesota."

It probably helped that, in his evaluation of Grant, Finks further remarked to longtime Vikings player and brilliant talent evaluator Jerry Reichow that Bud Grant was "luckiest man I have ever seen." This observation may have been based upon the number of times Grant defeated Finks' teams in Canada.

Reichow also has fond memories of Jim Finks and speaks of him with great regard. He says, "Jim Finks is the best I have ever seen and the best football man I have ever been around." This is quite a statement from a man who has been connected with the NFL every day since he played for the Detroit Lions in 1956 over 50 years ago!

Longtime assistant coach under Grant and former head coach of the Vikings, Jerry Burns knew Jim Finks well and often played golf with the onetime general manager. "He had a personality at times like Van Brocklin," says Burns, "and he was a 'real tough guy' and a horse #%%# golfer."

But Burns is familiar with Finks' football prowess, alluding to the fact that the former athlete played before Unitas while with Pittsburgh. "He was very football centered, and he knew the game," says Burns. They had a great relationship and Burns shows nothing but respect for his friend and former Vikings general manager.

Community leader and former Viking Stu Voigt also speaks very highly of Jim Finks. "He was a great general manager and he knew football," says Voigt, a huge supporter of the work Finks did while with the Vikings.

Honesty, integrity, credibility—all were part of the package. Jim Finks' solid reputation as a great NFL administrator was widespread, not only while in Canada and with the Vikings, but also later with the Chicago Bears and the New Orleans Saints.

Finks resigned from the Vikings in the spring of 1974 over future ownership issues, and by the beginning of the fall season, he had joined the Chicago Bears.

Another unidentified person once said, "I can't imagine the number of championships the Vikings would have won if Finks and

Grant had stayed together." The statement takes nothing away from future administrators, but reflects on the beautiful seven-year marriage between Bud Grant and Jim Finks.

Finks was successful in Calgary, with the Vikings and Bears, and later with the Cubs baseball organization and the New Orleans Saints. He knew how to manage and he knew how to do it the right way. His history proclaims that he built perennial losers into winners and brought about a respect and dignity to organizations in the process.

An unknown source once gave a quote that sums up the executive career of Jim Finks. This individual said, "Jim Finks does not build teams. He builds organizations."

When Jim Finks left the Vikings in 1974, his departure made room for another administrator to take over major duties and responsibilities as the general manager of the Vikings.

At first, the new person was to have a small role, yet his authority grew over the years until he became one of the most powerful and entertaining executives in all of sports.

His name was Mike Lynn, and there aren't enough pages in this book or any other to totally describe his personality and passionate contributions to the game. "He called it "SHOWBIZ."

Former players who had to negotiate contracts with Mike Lynn describe the Vikings general manager in a rather uncomplimentary fashion, but those who contributed to the organization in off-the-field roles loved working for him.

He was a businessman and an extremely interesting personality. He had strong beliefs and was not fearful of exercising what he believed was best for the Minnesota Vikings football team. One of his staff members found out what Mike Lynn was like the hard way.

"WHO WASHED MY CAR? I WANT TO KNOW WHO WASHED MY CAR!"

Pat Leopold, a University of Minnesota student, was a young intern with the Vikings during Lynn's time in office. The above exclamation lent itself to a sleepless night and a terrifying meeting with the general manager.

Mike Lynn had been out of town on business and was arriving at the airport late in the afternoon. Leopold's boss had asked him to take Mike Lynn's car to the airport and leave it there for Lynn to pick up when he returned from his trip.

Leopold followed the instructions, but also added to them. Lynn's Sterling was in dire need of some tender loving care. So, on the way to the airport, Leopold drove it through a car wash and cleaned up the whole vehicle, inside and out. He thought the act would be a good way to impress the boss.

When the cleanup was finished, Leopold drove the car to the airport, rode back to the office with another employee, and went home. A call he received at his house that evening informed the intern of the following incident.

Mike Lynn had picked up his car at the airport, returned to Winter Park, and proceeded up and down the executive aisles, asking, "WHO WASHED MY CAR? I WANT TO KNOW WHO WASHED MY CAR!"

Leopold was advised that the tone of the boss' question was not good, and Lynn wanted to see him in his office at 9 a.m. the next morning. A sleepless night and a great deal of worry followed Leopold to the office the next morning.

At 9 a.m. he entered Mike Lynn's office with his boss, Sherm Pinkham. Upon entering, Lynn immediately asked Leopold, "DID YOU WASH MY CAR?" Leopold explained he thought he was doing Lynn a favor, and he would happily pay for any damage he caused.

Lynn then asked, "WHO GAVE YOU PERMISSION TO WASH MY CAR?" Leopold said he had decided to do it on his own and again repeated that he would pay for any damages to the car.

Lynn looked at him and said, "SO YOU TOOK MY CAR AND WASHED IT WITHOUT ANYONE'S PERMISSION. IS THAT RIGHT?" Leopold answered in the affirmative.

Mike Lynn smiled and told Pat Leopold he had a full-time job with the Vikings if he wanted it. Many years later, Leopold is still with the Vikings and is the coordinator of the Viking Children's Fund. He loves to tell the story as he shares his admiration for his former boss.

Mike Lynn is a fascinating person, to say the very least. He is not football educated and is the first to admit it. When Jerry Burns was the head coach of the Vikings, Lynn used to find ways to irritate him, though all in good fun. Burns says that Lynn would come into his office and diagram plays on the board, asking, "Coach, why don't we run something like … ?" Burns would look at him and reply something to the effect of, "Get the ##&% out of my office!" The two have great mutual respect for each other and laugh about those days when Lynn pretended to help with game plans.

Lynn's attitude differed from most general managers of professional football teams. "We are in the entertainment business," he used to say. "We are not in life-or-death situations. Showbiz."

While working toward obtaining a franchise in Memphis, Lynn became associated with Elvis Presley. He had thought the name and popularity of a country icon might help bring an NFL franchise to Memphis. It might have, too, if Elvis' manager, Colonel Parker, hadn't ended the relationship.

Regardless, Lynn enjoys telling people how Elvis almost attended a Vikings practice some years back. "During one of Elvis' last appearances in St. Paul, one of his front people called and asked if Elvis could come to the Vikings practice that day," Lynn recalls. He remembers responding to the request something to the effect of, "You have got to be crazy! The last thing we need is to have Elvis come tromping out onto the practice field!"

"Can you imagine what Bud Grant would have said?" Lynn continues, "It never happened, but it could have happened if I had said yes. But I don't think the coach would have been too happy with me." Elvis and the Purple? Maybe he should have granted the request. It would have been a great memory in franchise history.

Before joining the Vikings, Lynn was not connected to professional football in a team sense. He was, however, the leader of a group trying to obtain an NFL franchise in Memphis, Tennessee.

He headed an organization called Mid-South Sports, Inc. This group sponsored eight NFL preseason games, and was making a strong effort to bring a franchise to Memphis.

Lynn was a competent and diligent leader in his pursuit to obtain an NFL franchise. He founded the Chamber of Commerce Sports Committee, was chairman of the mayor's NFL Committee, and was appointed by the governor to represent Memphis and the state of Tennessee in all communications with the NFL.

At the same time, Lynn was also serving as chief executive officer of the Memphis American Basketball Association Team.

Lynn ended his quest for an NFL franchise when, despite his objections, the city chose to go with a World Football League team rather than waiting for the NFL. Disappointed in the city's decision, he resigned his position. His interest in the NFL, however, didn't end in Memphis.

Lynn wrote a letter to Max Winter expressing interest in joining the Vikings. Shortly after, he got a reply indicating that he did not have the proper qualifications for the job. Two weeks later, however, Max Winter called him. He wanted to meet to discuss the letter further. After the meeting, Lynn was hired as the assistant to the president, and the following year he was named general manager of the Minnesota Vikings.

He was an entertaining administrator and always made good press. "You never had to worry about being on the front page of the sports page when Mike Lynn was around," said Fred Zamberletti. Mike Lynn would find a way to get you there.

The press once criticized him for flying a plane with team pilots at the team's expense to a fancy California clothing store and purchasing a dozen or so $2,000 suits.

"Never happened," said Lynn, "and I was never in the store where I allegedly flew and made the purchase. But there is something I did the media never found out about."

Mike Lynn had a family pet, a Great Dane, at his home in Memphis. He had planned to fly the dog to the Twin Cities to be with his family. Because the temperature had dropped, the airlines would not fly the pet to the Cities, so Lynn dispatched the Vikings' pilots to Memphis to fly their dog to Minnesota.

"The media would have loved to have found out about that one," laughs Lynn. It most certainly would have made for good reading if they had.

During all his years with the Vikings, Mike Lynn had one goal in mind and never drifted off course. That goal was to get to the Super Bowl and win it. The ultimate in championships did not occur for the Vikings, but Lynn never let up in his pursuit of the NFL dream while he managed the front office.

Recently, ESPN aired a program entitled "The Ten Worst Trades in Sports History." Featured on the program was the infamous Herschel Walker trade made by Mike Lynn with the Dallas Cowboys.

It will probably go down in history as one of the worst professional sports trades ever, not only according to Vikings fans, but to anyone with any type of sports interest. Common sense would dictate that trades are only bad when they don't work out. And this one certainly didn't. At the beginning, however, it looked to be a grand move on the part of the Vikings.

Fans listening to the radio that fateful afternoon may recall Brent Musburger announcing the trade, saying something to the effect of, "The Vikings and the Cowboys made a trade today ... and folks, it was a blockbuster!" Few knew the details for some time after the trade, but what he didn't say was ... "Herschel Walker goes to the Vikings for five players and nine draft choices," or something close to that number ... around 14 players!

Restrictions on players and draft choices made the trade very complicated. In any event, it was the trade of the decade, or maybe better said, decades. Knowing the potential of what Herschel Walker was capable of bringing to the Vikings, many would have made the trade, just perhaps not for so many high draft choices.

Former head coach Jerry Burns remembers the Vikings' locker room atmosphere after the announcement of the trade. The athletes were in shock, as several players from the current team were leaving.

But Mike Lynn wanted to win, and he was of the opinion Walker would be the missing key to winning a Super Bowl. It was his sole motivation behind the trade with Dallas.

When the trade was first announced, there probably wasn't a fan in the state of Minnesota who was not excited about the Vikings' future. Herschel Walker was coming to the Minnesota Vikings! The great back from Georgia and the Cowboys would don the purple in the Twin Cities, taking the team, community, state, and region to the Promised Land.

Few Vikings fans doubted that it was a great trade, and the doubters all but changed their minds the first time Walker touched the football. Mark Thielen, a longtime passionate Vikings fan, recalls the announcement. "I was excited about the trade. I never thought about the number of players involved in the deal, because we were getting Herschel Walker," says Thielen. "He was a team-changing player. There was never a worry. This guy was Herschel Walker, and after the first game, we couldn't wait until next week! He was going to put us back on the map."

The first game reiterated everything the trade was meant to accomplish. From the opening kickoff against the Packers at the Metrodome, the trade looked to be a gem.

Walker grabbed the ball deep in Vikings territory and streaked up the field across the 50-yard line before he was tripped up just short of the end zone. Had he taken that kickoff the distance, the roars inside the dome may have crumpled the roof, sending the state into the most frenzied uproar since "Two Minute" Tommy Kramer hit Ahmad Rashad on the last play of a game against Cleveland in 1980 to send the Vikings to the playoffs. The old Met Stadium has long since been torn down, and on the site now rests the world-famous Mall of America. But if you pay close attention in the quiet of the night, you can still hear the roar of fans who watched as Rashad caught Kramer's pass and backed into the end zone. The sounds are still there. You just have to listen carefully for them.

The rest of the Vikings-Packers game was all Herschel Walker. He was unstoppable, rushing the ball for over 150 yards. Mike Lynn missed the chance of a lifetime after Herschel's first day with the Purple. He should have announced himself as an immediate candidate for sainthood. He would have been granted it in a heartbeat.

But it was never meant to be. "If the Vikings had made it to the Super Bowl that year and won, it would have been one of the greatest trades ever made," said Lynn. "If the Vikings had made it to the Super Bowl and lost, the trade would have still been OK. But it turned out to be a train wreck."

Maybe the trade just never had a chance to succeed. Expectations from the very beginning were too high, and nothing short of winning the Super Bowl would have been considered a success. And it certainly was not Herschel's fault. He didn't make the trade. He didn't have anything to do with it.

Zamberletti has analyzed the trade and all of its ramifications pretty well. "If Herschel Walker had come in here as a second- or third-round draft choice, he would have gone down in Viking history as a great running back, but because of the high expectations, his time here is looked upon as being negative."

Walker took terrible abuse from the fans as the trade turned to disaster. But Jerry Burns and Mike Lynn speak of Walker with great passion.

"He came to me and said he would do anything to help the team win," said Jerry Burns. He told Burns to put him on special teams or give him any assignment. He just wanted to help in any way possible. He was a great man of character and one worthy of respect.

Lynn says Walker "was a wonderful person and a charming man. He could have become the first black president of the United States had he wanted to take his career in that direction." But pro football in purple just didn't work out.

Would Mike Lynn make the trade again without knowing the ultimate results? "Oh yeah!" exclaims Lynn.

Lynn speaks of a thorough evaluation that had taken place at the end of the previous season. He says most years the evaluation would address sometimes as many as "seven, eight, 10 needs of the team." But this time, that was not the case.

The Vikings had nine players in the pro bowl that year, were within one play of making it to the Super Bowl, and the only identifiable need, according to Lynn, was getting the "big back."

In Lynn's mind, the Vikings' mission was to win the Super Bowl. He was convinced it was perhaps the Vikings' last chance to utilize the great strengths of the current team, and he strongly believed the only thing the Vikings needed to accomplish his goal was a "big back." With a great college and professional reputation, Herschel Walker was that great, power-driving runner who could put it all together for a "last run." But it didn't work out.

Mike Lynn was criticized greatly through the years for the trade. The general manager was also criticized for his tough negotiation standards with many of the players. He had a role to fill and, from some points of view, did it with little praise and acclimation.

However, some players have spoken very highly of Mike Lynn, and practically everyone who worked for him in a non-player capacity loved doing so. Lynn was a front-office personality in the literal sense of the word. He rarely went to training camp and he rarely went to the practice field. He ran the front office.

He says his tough contract negotiations centered around the fact that the Vikings were a small-market team owned by a small group of owners who could not compete financially with others within the NFL, including Lamar Hunt, then-owner of the Kansas City Chiefs.

As the mid-'80s approached, Lynn began to obtain more power in the organization. The ownership group was down to three, and Lynn was put in total control by a two-thirds majority vote. He was the decision maker and ran the Vikings.

As he worked to find the secret to winning, Lynn tried many approaches. He even took the team out west on a "bonding trip" to a retreat haven called Pecos River. A few days away from the spotlight would give the players time to get closer to one another. Team leadership had agreed to the trip after a pre-visit. Interesting to many and criticized by others, the experimental journey was all part of Lynn's relentless desire to produce winners on the field.

During the trip, some of the athletes were surprised to hear what Lynn had done behind the scenes to help out others. At a group bonding session, one player said that the general manager had helped him out of a tough court situation and had the judge release the player to his custody. Lynn's actions were instrumental in assisting the player through one of the most difficult times of his life.

One of the coaches told the group that Lynn had helped out a seriously ill coach by extending his contract solely as a gesture to assist the family, even though he knew the man wouldn't be coaching anymore.

Few ever heard what Lynn did behind the scenes while with the organization. "We made a concentrated effort to connect to the community," says Lynn. "We didn't do it for publicity. It wasn't our purpose to publicize our good deeds."

The Vikings' community work at the time was very much underplayed. Lynn says, "If we did something good, we didn't toot our own horns about it. ... Let's just do it and feel good that we are helping. ... If there were some kids that were sick and we could arrange for players to visit and make their lives happier ... we just did it."

During Lynn's time in office, the Vikings worked closely with the University of Minnesota Children's Hospital, Fairview, and continue to do so to this day. The Vikings' commitment to contributing money for research of childhood diseases through the years is quietly legendary.

Lynn's impact on football went far beyond his position as general manager of the Minnesota Vikings. Few ever knew of his expansive role in NFL matters. He never talked about it much, but estimates that about 30 to 40 percent of his time was spent on league issues and decisions.

Mike Lynn had been approached by Pete Rozelle, NFL Commissioner, to become heavily involved in all aspects of the operations of the league. He was appointed to several key committees, which made great demands on his time.

Lynn recalls a phone call one morning from Governor Rudy Perpich's chief of staff. He was advised that the governor wanted to see him at 3:00 that afternoon. It was a freezing day in the Twin Cities and little parking surrounded the capitol. Lynn had a desk full of work, so he declined the request, saying he wouldn't be able to make the meeting.

A few minutes later he received a second call from the chief of staff to inform him if he did not plan to attend, the Minnesota State Highway Patrol would escort him to the Governor's office.

At the 3 p.m. meeting, Governor Perpich told Lynn there was going to be a press conference at 3:30 that afternoon. The topic? The State of Minnesota was going to make a bid for the Super Bowl to be played in Minnesota.

Upon hearing what the governor had in mind, Lynn tried to show the utmost respect when he exclaimed something to the effect of, "Are you absolutely crazy? There is absolutely no chance of the NFL owners voting to bring a Super Bowl to a cold-weather city."

However, the governor had a plan for Mr. Lynn. He wanted the general manager to carry his message to the NFL owners and make it happen. Lynn thought it was a terrible idea and sneaked out the back door to avoid the press conference. He was disappointed later when he learned of the "beating" the governor took by the press and others for such an outrageous thought process. "It was brutal, the way they treated him," recalls Lynn.

These were times in Minnesota political history when the media was extremely unkind to Rudy Perpich, the highest elected state official, and often referred to him as "Governor Goofy." It was that bad.

Lynn became so angry over the media's treatment that he went out in personal pursuit of the championship game. Lynn's first move in support of the governor's wishes to bring a Super Bowl to Minnesota was a call to Pete Rozelle, asking him to put the issue on the next owner meeting's agenda.

He used the logic that, before merging with the American Football League, many of the great NFL championship games were played in the cold. He noted that warm-weather Super Bowls were merely a byproduct of the merger and proposed that every seven years the Super Bowl be in a "Northern Tier."

The first time the owners gave the matter consideration, only 15 were in favor of the idea. Needing a 75-percent majority of the 28 owners to vote in the affirmative, Lynn was woefully short. The press had another field day, reporting that the NFL "soundly defeated" the idea, and essentially mocked the concept.

No one realized, however, that they were dealing with Mike Lynn. At the next owner's meeting, a vote was taken to approve Miami and New Orleans as future host cities for the Super Bowl. Lynn contacted every owner who had originally backed his plan and they were united. He was therefore successful in blocking approval for future Super Bowls in Miami and New Orleans. Now, the NFL was in a real quandary and Lynn's "Northern Tier" was being carefully considered.

Rozelle was furious. The owners were hopelessly deadlocked and a 75-percent majority would not approve a warm city, let alone a cold-weather city.

Lynn refused to release the votes unless he got his way. He had control and won out. The owners eventually voted to play in a "Northern Tier" city every seven years. Many bids were taken from the "Northern Tier" cities, which were finally trimmed down to Minnesota and Seattle.

Seattle looked to be the favorite, since its climate was certainly more favorable than that of Minnesota during Super Bowl time. And they remained the favorite—at least until Lynn stood up and spoke passionately to the owners. He told Rudy Perpich's story. He explained that the governor had come up with the idea and had

Regardless of the circumstances, Mike Lynn always managed to make his time as general manager of the Vikings interesting.
*Photo courtesy of the Minnesota Vikings*

been disrespected by the media and treated poorly by the state. He pronounced to the owners, "Give this man back his dignity" and sat down.

Philadelphia Eagles owner Norman Braman looked over at Lynn and said, "You got yourself a Super Bowl!" And the rest is history. The Super Bowl was played in Minneapolis, Minnesota, at the Metrodome on January 26, 1992, in the middle of winter!

Lynn left the Vikings in 1991 and retired from pro football. His father died at the age of 47 and the general manager did not want a short future once he finally left the game. The long hours and many years away from home were taking their toll and it was time to start living leisurely.

From the age of 55 to 65 he truly enjoyed life, traveling and doing whatever he wanted to do. At the age of 65 he faced serious health problems, but is doing well now. He spends about half of his time at the Oxford University Club in Oxford, Mississippi, and the other half developing an incredible tourist area in Holly Springs, Mississippi, where he resides.

Although many miles now separate him from Winter Park, a big part of Mike's heart will always be purple. As Mike Lynn looks back on his career with the Vikings, he speaks of only one regret. It might come as a surprise to some, especially those who locked horns with him during contract time. "I regret not taking care of Bill Brown when it came to his contract," Lynn says. He thought a lot of Brown and to this day wishes he had handled things differently. "I should have given him what he wanted. It has always bothered me."

Lynn enjoyed the control and the power to make things happen, like when Bears coach Mike Ditka complained that the Metrodome was a poor excuse for a football field and called it something like … a "barnyard and a place to roller skate."

Those who attended the next game against the Bears still remember the huge, fake cattle, farm scenes, and barnyard characters on the sidelines, along with the roller skaters that greeted Ditka and the Bears as they entered the "barnyard arena." Mike Lynn was on center stage and loved every minute of it.

Mary Nevers, a longtime Vikings receptionist deeply loyal to the organization, speaks highly of Mike Lynn. She said that he always seemed to find a way to keep things interesting. He would often walk by her desk in the lobby at Winter Park and say, "I think I'll go in the back and stir things up a little." That was Mike Lynn. He had the power to do it and he often did just that.

Many staff say that Lynn took the staff on trips during the off-season and that the organization was very close during his tenure as general manager.

Winning on Sunday afternoon was the most important aspect of his job and he worked at it endlessly. But second on his agenda and very important to Mike Lynn was stability in the organization. He wanted the staff to be comfortable and like a family, and he worked hard at that aspect of his job as well.

He was not a football man. He was a businessman in a football town and arena, and he thrived on it every minute of every single day. And he went about it in a flamboyant manner. He was Mike Lynn, like him or not. He ran the Vikings for many years and he sure was entertaining!

After one of the worst days in Minnesota Vikings history, Jeff Diamond began working for the organization. Not many people would like to begin their first day on the job following a day of infamy. But Jeff Diamond did exactly that.

That fateful Sunday in early January of 1976 will forever haunt the organization and Vikings faithful as perhaps the most ugly day of devastation in the 46-year history of the franchise.

Some will proclaim with little argument from others that the 1975 Vikings may have been the best ever, which made it so difficult to accept what occurred in the team's playoff game against Dallas.

The ruin that took place at the old Metropolitan Stadium was initiated by the Cowboys and enhanced by an officiating crew that failed to call an offensive pass interference on Dallas in the closing seconds of the game, ending the Purple's quest for yet another Super Bowl.

It is hard to understand how, over 46 seasons with hundreds of games and thousands of officials' decisions, one occurrence on the field lasting only a matter of a few seconds can last in the memory of each Vikings fan for a lifetime.

When asked to talk about the 1976 playoff game against Dallas, there is notable anger in the voice of Vikings fan Mark Thielen. "Tell you about it? I'll tell you about it," he replies in a tone reflecting 30 years of pent-up anger and hostility. "You couldn't walk up to any fan who has followed Vikings football and not get a strong reaction to what happened in that game."

Continues Thielen, "It was the greatest robbery of all time. There is nothing to compare to what Pearson did in that game. When it happened, I just looked around at the people with me, and no one could believe what they had just seen. The thought was, 'This didn't happen!'"

Fans might remember one popular Vikings merchandise item: a foam purple brick. "After what had occurred, I picked up that Vikings brick and threw it and kicked it all over the room," Thielen recalls. "I remember thinking as I watched the television, 'They are going to change this ... they are going to change this.' But they never did."

Thielen goes on to talk about the animation associated with that infamous Minnesota-Dallas playoff game. "If you were going to walk up to someone who was sitting quietly in a chair and ask them to recall their memories of the game, you would likely get a reaction of great anger."

Thielen says they might reply, "Why did you have to do this to me? Why did you have to bring this up, to make me talk about something so painful?"

Mark Thielen has a friend whose father had a mild heart attack immediately after the infamous play sunk the Vikings' Super Bowl hopes. The man went to the doctor right after the game and was given treatment for his condition. In his rehabilitation instructions, the doctor forbid the patient from watching or listening to any future Vikings football games until his condition improved. The game was that devastating.

Another Vikings fan, Kim Lokken, remembers the game as if it were a nightmare. "It was just like the referees wanted Dallas to win the game," says Lokken. "It was so blatant that Pearson pushed off. He knocked Wright right to the ground! Everyone saw it and the pictures in the newspapers the following day showed clearly what had happened."

Kim Lokken also vividly remembers the play before Pearson's touchdown. "That was another bad officials' call, when Pearson was not ruled out of bounds near the 50-yard line on a pass from Staubach," says Lokken.

"I was down near the field and ready to go out and tear down the goal posts after the Vikings' victory. And then it happened. I couldn't believe it. Everyone was in total disbelief. I remember looking up at the scoreboard and saw it to be true," a disheartened Kim Lokken says, reliving the pain over 30 years later.

"It was such a good team that won so frequently that it made losses very hard to except," says Fred Zamberletti. "The expectations were there to win. There were very hearty fans in the stands. There were many World War II veterans with kids that grew up remembering the earlier glory days of the Vikings. It was outside and there was great pride in the toughness of the conditions, and the fans were tough, hard-nosed people."

And, to make matters worse, "the Vikings had the game won," Zamberletti recalls.

He continues, "There were three things that occurred in the game that stand out. First, the play before, Drew Pearson caught a pass and came down out of bounds and this also was not called by the officials. Secondly, on the final play pass by Staubach, the ball was dribbled back to him by the center, and he was still able to scoop it up and throw the pass. And thirdly, the completion took place after Pearson pushed Vikings defender Nate Wright to the ground. Nate Wright went down like he had been shot. Pearson was a basketball player and used his skills to push off.

"But the worst part of the day for the Vikings came later when it was learned that Fran Tarkenton's father had died that Sunday. So it was a double hurt," said Zamberletti. It was, without question, one of the darkest days in Minnesota Vikings history.

Led by the great Fran Tarkenton, the Vikings had executed a lengthy ball-control drive in the waning moments of the game to take the lead and assumed victory. But a final gasp, a desperate play of last resort, collapsed the Vikings' hopes and season.

Dallas Cowboy quarterback Roger Staubach launched the ball about as far down the field as possible in his last second "Hail Mary" attempt to retain the lead. Cowboy receiver Drew Pearson raced for the ball and, in his furious attempt to make the catch, pushed Vikings defensive back Nate Wright to the ground. He then caught the pass and essentially walked untouched into the end zone.

It was a flagrant foul by Pearson, but no flag was thrown. Pearson's act bordered on criminal. The officials should have called a penalty, jumped up and down, and demanded that Pearson be banned from ever playing or watching another football game for life. They should have, yet they never did. The field was clear without a trace of yellow on the ground.

If every fan in the stands had possessed a penalty flag that Sunday afternoon at the Met, 47,000 would have showered their way onto the playing field. But they didn't. The season was over and the moment would linger on in the days, the months, and the years ahead, forever in the hearts of those cheering for the Purple.

The Vikings lost on that sorry day at Metropolitan Stadium, an official was hit in the head by a bottle thrown by a berserk fan, and the aftermath was ugly. Fights occurred in the stands, as if the spectators had turned on each other in some bizarre form of retaliation over what had occurred right before their very eyes.

And, on the very next day, intern Jeff Diamond reported for his very first day with the Minnesota Vikings.

"The place was like a morgue," he recalled. Everyone was in a depressed state." His career with the Vikings got off to a rough start due to the disaster at the Met, but the next year would be another great one for the Vikings. In some ways, it was almost too much glory for Diamond to take on at the beginning of his career.

The Vikings lost to Dallas on that fateful Sunday, but the next year's team was also among the NFL elite. It was an incredible season as the Vikings went on to their fourth Super Bowl.

Ironically, it was the last trip to Super Bowl Sunday for the Vikings and Jeff Diamond, until the latter of the two left the franchise for the Tennessee Titans, who then went to the championship game during Diamond's first year as president with the team.

For a young man from the Twin Cities who grew up in love with the Minnesota Vikings, to be hired by the team right out of the University of Minnesota and to remain with the franchise for the next 23 years can only be remembered as a "dream come true."

Diamond speaks with great loyalty to the organization where he spent over two decades. He loved his job and the people he worked with every day. And he always remembered the great moments in Vikings history—like the time Joe Kapp ran over a Rams defensive back and crashed into the end zone in the Vikings' great playoff victory in 1969—as a fan first, rather than an employee.

Jeff Diamond wore many hats during those 23 years, and even wrote *The First Fifteen Years*, a book on the Vikings. When Mike Lynn resigned, Diamond took over most of the general manager duties for the team, which included player contract negotiations and trade initiation and execution. He was also involved in the football side of business within the franchise.

"There was a group of people in the organization that were together for such a long time and had so much success," says Diamond. His words reiterate his love for the Vikings and express the good fortune he believed he had while part of their glory years.

Diamond has a great sense of humor and even appreciated some frustrating moments within the organization. He was in charge of a couple trips the team took to Europe to play NFL preseason games. The arrangements for the game were often challenging, to say the least.

Diamond recalls discussing an upcoming game with the team's European host group. The Vikings needed room in the press box for their coaches during the game, which was creating a major problem. Diamond could not get his message across to the group, since they could not understand why he wanted the coaches in the press box in the first place.

After several minutes of debating the issue and explaining the Vikings' needs, an understanding was finally reached without any more confusion. Once the host group understood that Diamond was talking about the players' coaches, not the Vikings' motor coaches, all was resolved quickly.

Jeff Diamond worked hard during his tenure with the Minnesota Vikings and learned the business very well. He was well liked by the coaches, players, and those people he communicated with on a daily basis. His work was so well received that, in 1999, he was named NFL Executive of the Year—quite an honor for a man employed by his hometown team.

His gratefulness to the organization can easily be summed up by the following words. "They hold a special place in my heart," says Diamond. "It is a professional organization and a professional operation. It has been a winning team and has done it the right way. It has been a team built in the highest of esteem."

Among many other duties and responsibilities during his proud and glorious years with the Vikings, Jeff Diamond was a fan, intern, book writer, and public relations executive. He even filled the role of general manager. And, on his very last day as he left his office and the Vikings, the man he had such great admiration for was there to say goodbye and wish him well—Bud Grant.

"The first time I met Bud I was scared to death of him," says Diamond. "I had such great respect for him. He was always in control. He was so fair and so consistent, and such a great judge of character and people. He was such a good person."

Continues Diamond, "I saw his emotion when he left the team and at his Pro Football Hall of Fame induction. He was a wonderful family man and was so much about his family. And he was such a great coach."

After 23 years, leaving the Vikings was very difficult for Jeff Diamond. Packing up his personal belongings and preparing to leave his office for the final time was quite emotional, but Grant's presence helped.

"He came down to my office to see me and say goodbye," says Diamond. "He told me, 'Life in pro sports is difficult and you have had a great run here.' It just meant so much to me that Bud was there that night."

Diamond now lives in Nashville. He had a successful run for five years as the president of the Tennessee Titans and is now the chief executive officer of the Ingram Consulting Group.

He does work for the National Hockey League's Nashville Predators, is working toward getting a new stadium for the Nashville Sounds minor-league baseball team, and is helping to develop some golf courses. He is also involved in radio with both the NFL and ESPN and works with a few NFL teams on corporate partnerships. Needless to say, Jeff Diamond remains a busy and highly sought after, competent executive.

During Diamond's last several years in a role similar to a general manager, the Vikings' front person in an ownership position was Roger Headrick. Headrick had come to the Vikings as an owner of the organization and took over leadership after the departure of Mike Lynn.

Headrick was from the corporate world, having left the Pillsbury Corporation after a company buyout. Although he had never been involved in professional sports, he was once offered a job in player personnel with the Baltimore Orioles organization. His college baseball background and friendship with a one-time competitor on the field had presented the opportunity.

The job was only half of what he was already earning financially with the Exxon Corporation, so he decided to stay in the business field. This decision later gave Headrick the chance to state, tongue in cheek, "It was better to start at the top of an organization than at the bottom." And he was able to do just this with the Minnesota Vikings.

Mike Lynn, Headrick's neighbor, introduced Headrick's interest in an ownership role with the Vikings, as Lynn was looking toward the new World Football League and bowing out of the organization.

Roger Headrick took over the Vikings' day-to-day operations and ran the franchise like a business. He made many changes in formal structure and essentially set up the organization to operate as three entities, which consisted of research, manufacturing, and everything else.

The new structure created an interesting analogy to the "reality" of corporate business. The research side included the scouting department, responsible for identifying and finding players. The manufacturing side of the business was the coaching staff, responsible for taking the ingredients and making them into a team. The rest of the operation consisted of all remaining parts of the organization.

Headrick, Diamond, and then head coach Dennis Green worked well together and often divided the budget up together as if they were "slicing up a pizza," giving all areas their proper shares. Diamond worked out the contracts, Green did the fieldwork, and Headrick oversaw the operation. Each proved very successful in his responsibility.

Headrick has a unique way of looking at the CEO position of an NFL franchise. "It has the high of highs and the low of lows," he says. "If you win, you get an A grade and if you lose, you get an F. But the job was interesting and very exciting. The one thing that few people really understand about football is that everyone else in every other organization is also trying to win."

And, as Bud Grant has often said, "Sometimes they are just better than us."

"'Win on the field and pay the bills' is a big part of pro football and the reality of running a franchise," says Headrick. He was well trained in the business part of his role and utilized other expertise within the organization to deliver the field product.

When it comes to that expertise, Roger Headrick is passionate and forever complimentary regarding the Vikings' scouting area—research, as he calls it. He has incredibly high opinions of longtime Vikings personnel Paul Wiggin, Frank Gilliam, Jerry Reichow, and Scott Studwell.

"They have been quality people who have gone out and found the talent and have been the essence of the Vikings," says Headrick. "When you look at longtime, successful organizations in professional football, you will find they have had coaches in place for long periods of time and scouting staff that have brought in the players they needed."

Headrick was convinced to hire Denny Green because of his impressive reputation in both the college and professional ranks. He received great recommendations from such icons as Bill Walsh and Dick Vermeil as to Green's coaching and organizational skills. And Green's success on the field proved it to be a good decision.

During his leadership role with the Vikings, Roger Headrick was most proud of starting the organization's player development department. He picked former Viking Leo Lewis to head up the responsibility. Most teams include this as a part of their operations today.

Leo Lewis was to develop the department, which would eventually work with players in four areas: first, to convince and assist players to complete their education; second, to assist them in becoming financially intelligent by creating a good fiscal plan; third, to aid them in finding positive activities to take part in the off-season; and lastly, to think about life after their careers were over. Such development is crucial for anyone's future, and Lewis and Headrick felt the goals were especially important for Minnesota Vikings athletes.

Headrick came to the Vikings with great skills in marketing and finance. He was a legitimate corporate executive and understood leadership. Headrick was born in West Orange, New Jersey, and attended Williams College, receiving a BA degree and an MBA from Columbia University.

Before taking over his powerful role with the Vikings, he had held top management positions at the Exxon Corporation and also with The Pillsbury Company. He was in charge of the Purple and performed well for slightly less than a decade of their history.

He was brilliant in the financial sense of the word, and took the Vikings in the right direction. At the end of his tenure, an unpleasant separation from other Vikings owners led to a failed attempt to buy the franchise with his own ownership group. But Roger Headrick was a good man and a sound business executive. He cared about the people who worked for him and continues to praise their accomplishments.

As he looks back on his years with the Vikings, the only decision he regrets was not taking Warren Sapp in the NFL Draft when he had the opportunity. The Vikings had earlier traded Chris Doleman to Atlanta for draft picks, one of them a first rounder. Sapp was on the board and the Vikings passed on him. "Can you imagine the Vikings' future with Sapp and John Randle together?" asks Headrick.

He had a good run as the CEO of the Vikings and made many sound business decisions. Roger Headrick is a professional's professional. He should be proud of his accomplishments as the leader of the Minnesota Vikings. "I did the best I could," says Headrick. "It was a lot of fun!"

As the '90s elapsed and Green became a perennial winner, he wanted more control over football operations. Green, like many other successful and powerful NFL coaches, thrived on his coaching role as well as some general manager duties within the operation. He wanted total control, and in many respects, it is understandable.

In 1998, the beginning of some major changes in Vikings history occurred when Red McCombs of San Antonio, Texas, purchased the team. McCombs, a self-made millionaire, built an automotive business from the ground up to a major corporation.

Successful in many other ventures, including other professional sports franchises, McCombs came to the Twin Cities under the proclamation of "PURPLE PRIDE, PURPLE PRIDE." Almost as if ownership and business were the last thing on his mind, winning was on the front burner. But McCombs was a businessman first and demonstrated it throughout most of his tenure with the team.

Winning exploded onto the scene with McCombs' first team in 1998, as the Purple finished an amazing season with a 15-1 regular-season record only to be upset in the playoffs. This, too, was a horrendous loss that still finds its way onto local sports pages and columns on a fairly routine basis, especially when things aren't glowing with perfection for the men of Winter Park.

After the shocking defeat, the Vikings made some major changes in the front office. Green was able to capture the power he coveted and became the heart and soul of all personnel decisions, which essentially ended Jeff Diamond's reign with the franchise.

As mentioned previously, however, Diamond went on to great success shortly thereafter. His career began with a trip to the Super Bowl with the Vikings in 1976. His next trip there would be some 24 years later with a different team, the Tennessee Titans. Diamond wouldn't be an intern during this trip; he would be the president of the NFL team.

When Dennis Green left the organization toward the conclusion of the 2001 season, the front office again adjusted, and power was spread out among several people with specialized backgrounds and expertise.

Mike Tice was the head coach for the next four years and shared overall personnel decisions with proficient individuals in the areas of contracts and player personnel. People like Rob Brzezinski, Jerry Reichow, Frank Gilliam, Scott Studwell, and Paul Wiggin developed sound leadership and made cooperative decisions for the Vikings.

But changes occurred once more in 2005 and are currently stabilized as the new regime begins to take full control of the franchise. A new coaching staff has taken the field and the Wilf family ownership group has moved into the front office at Winter Park, ready to manage the Minnesota Vikings football team.

Success on the field still is and always will be a high priority for the new ownership. The front office looks toward the Purple winning in Vikings fashion and tradition. The expectations are high, and also looming out on the horizon is a controversial issue not yet resolved, an issue perhaps bigger than most the Vikings have faced in their four-plus decades of operation—a new Vikings stadium. Regardless of what happens, though, the front office and ownership look toward the Purple to continue in the traditional Vikings fashion.

Proud ownership, competent leaders, great coaches, and legendary players have filled the Minnesota region with years of glory and tradition. Although the report card will always reflect the results of what occurs on the field, those behind the scenes in THE FRONT OFFICE sure make it all interesting.

# 5

# COMMUNITY CONNECTION

"WHAT TYPE OF PROTECTION are you going to use on this play?" If one were to take a close look at what is really important in life, perhaps this question posed by a Minnesota Viking notable to a little boy with cerebral palsy was as important as anything accomplished during the entire football season.

The passion, caring, and heartfelt commitment by Brad Childress, head coach of the Minnesota Vikings football team, to aid a physically challenged child will likely last in Chad Knapp's memory for a lifetime.

Taking time out from a busy schedule to help enhance the life of a young boy with a devastating disease keeps Brad Childress' priorities in the right place and symbolizes the importance of the Minnesota Vikings' dedication to aiding others less fortunate through connecting with the community as often as possible.

The Vikings demonstrate their winning presence in the community in a heartwarming and inspirational fashion. This is the other side of football for the Minnesota Vikings—the side that graduates understanding and love in ways almost unimaginable unless personally witnessed.

Fans, players, coaches, owners, administrators, and the public in general seem to be fixated on the NFL and what occurs on the field in primetime throughout the fall and winter months. Winning and losing and how either is accomplished have captured the imaginations and hearts of football followers. There appears to be a need to focus on whether those in purple, green and gold, black and silver, or those named Colts, Bengals, Bears, Rams, or Saints win or lose, and rarely do the interested observers look deeper into what is really occurring in an organization. "Commitment to Excellence" is common in locker-room lingo and lore, with the ultimate focus on winning.

But in the hearts of the Purple, winning is also brought about in many other ways. And it is often special and rarely forgotten. The Vikings' community connection is subtle and infrequently noted, but deeply appreciated by its recipients.

A story of long tradition, this relationship is worthy of significant recognition and acclaim. The Vikings' community connection should be acknowledged and praised for its incredible passion, commitment, and deep allegiance to assist others in need.

The public judges what is happening in professional sports and local franchises by what is written on the sports pages, broadcast on the evening news, or talked about in endless fashion on radio talk shows. Often an individual event, incident, or wrongdoing floods a perspective with ugly or bad press, engrossing an organization with devastating, long-lasting effects. Some community leaders and organizations outside the violent world of professional football, however, likely see it differently and recognize the importance of a professional football team's dedication off the playing field.

This very special kind of dedication was witnessed when the Minnesota Vikings visited Catholic Charities' St. Joseph's Home for Children on September 15, 2006, when the Vikings and Minneapolis Police Department hosted a "Football and Life" clinic.

Mark Klukow was coordinator for the Minneapolis Police Department. "The entire Viking organization was very positive in working with the police and the kids," says Klukow. "We weren't sure how we were going to be received. We are the ones who bring the children off the street or from their homes to St. Joe's. It was great to go there with the Vikings and be treated so well by everyone. All of the officers thought it was a great experience."

"Football and Life" began with a cold call from the Minneapolis Police Department to Brad Madson, director of community relations for the Vikings. The call was all that was needed for the Minnesota Vikings to respond and assist in this wonderful program for both children at St. Joseph's Home For Children and at-risk youngsters in the community.

It was an incredible event as the Vikings and the police joined forces to kick off the clinic at St. Joe's. Minneapolis police officers and Vikings players supervised the youngsters who practiced football drills and learned about teamwork and respect.

Klukow mentions that the Vikings donated 1,000 footballs at "Football and Life" to the police department. The footballs were put to good use during the fall season, when the police department used them to interact with individuals in high-risk neighborhoods in an attempt to bridge the gap often found between police officers and the community. "We would have 100 footballs in the back of our squad cars, and we would block off the streets of a neighborhood and play football with the kids," says Klukow. "At the end, we would give them each a football." By breaking down those barriers, the police also used the effort as a recruiting measure, "to help grow our future police force with local students."

The clinic was held at St. Joseph's Home for Children, which cares for children who are in crisis and makes certain their immediate needs are carefully looked at and addressed. Providing shelter and stability, the program offers methods for long-term solutions for the children's emotional and behavioral issues.

A division of Catholic Charities of St. Paul and Minneapolis, St. Joseph's Home for Children specializes in assessment and crisis interventions and residential programming. It deals extensively with children who have severe emotional and behavioral problems. More than 2,000 youth are served each year.

"Our children, typically when they go to sleep at night, tend to think about one of two things," says Mary Schoelch, volunteer coordinator at St. Joseph's Home for Children. "They will either think about the great sadness that has brought them to St. Joe's or they will think about the events of the day. And what makes this so special is spending time with police officers and Vikings players who are affirming of the kids, and will tell them—like Tarvaris Jackson might say to a seven-year-old, 'I love how you caught that pass,' or another of the players might say, 'You are a great receiver and you are just a really great athlete and I love to be with you.'

"These kinds of things are going to be remembered by these kids for the rest of their lives. It is an opportunity to be affirmed and to show off what they can do to be thought of as special. And when these kids drop off to sleep tonight here at St. Joe's, I can guarantee you that all are going to be thinking about the connection they had with the Vikings and police officers."

These children's memories of their role models are what make the event so special. And a warm smile, if it comes to the face of even one child preparing for bedtime at St. Joseph's Home for Children, makes it even more extraordinary.

"That's what makes these events so meaningful and special," says Schoelch, who truly understands the importance of such a valuable community connection. "We look at the individual players as they look at the kids—on a case-by-case basis. There are some absolutely wonderful, superb, caring, great kids here at St. Joseph's Home for Children. And there are some tremendous Vikings players who come and spend time with our kids and who have given of themselves individually. These are the things not routinely seen by the public."

Through the years, Schoelch has had the opportunity to see the effect the Minnesota Vikings players have had on the children, even though the organization is given little credit. While this work and dedicated commitment is not done for recognition or exposure, perhaps the results should be positively remembered and reported to the public in order to encourage others in and outside of the professional sports arena to also become involved.

"It saddens me in some respects, because many of the players will say they do not want a lot of publicity for what they do. It is more important for them to really form a connection with the kids. So here at Catholic Charities' St. Joseph's Home for Children, we deeply value the relationship," says Mary Schoelch. "I could wear a sandwich board walking up and down at the Mall of America talking about how terrific the Vikings organization has been. I don't think that an isolated incident should judge the entire organization."

The sandwich board would read, "Minnesota Vikings: more than you can imagine, better than you could possibly dream, tremendous players and great supporters of children and youth." What a statement about the organization, especially coming from a community expert who watches and observes the impact of their commitment on St. Joseph's Home for Children.

Little doubt remains about St. Joseph's Home for Children's feelings toward the Minnesota Vikings. The organization and individual players have been incredible in working with youngsters and bringing those special and so often desired smiles to their little faces.

Schoelch goes on to say, "When you look at the players having fun with the kids, it tells me they still have a kid in each one of them—that they can still relate and identify with our children and they have brought their empathy to us at St. Joe's. It is so tremendously genuine how they are connecting to our kids."

Spencer Johnson is 6-foot-3 and weighs 286 pounds. He is an Auburn University alum. But if you watch Johnson's interaction with the children, it is not his size, the Vikings jersey he proudly wears, or his prowess as an exceptional athlete that stands out around the children, but rather his infectious grin.

Whether at St. Joe's, Monroe Community School in St. Paul, or other community events at which Johnson gives his free time, this smile shows his commitment to make a day better for someone less fortunate.

"I have been doing this since high school," says the athlete. "It makes you feel good to see a smile on the children's faces. I will do it no matter what it is. I will do anything. In high school, I would take time with the kids that others were 'messing with.' I would play basketball with those kids and kind of take them under my wing. I did things for others in college as well. To see kids smile and happy makes me feel good—maybe better than the kids. It helps me to sleep at night and takes the pressure off."

Spencer Johnson is a great role model for children. His dedication to helping those in need is exciting and inspiring. He is a real credit to professional sports and demonstrates how important giving to others really is. He is proud to wear the Purple and the Purple are proud of him.

Vikings punter Chris Kluwe also has a clear understanding of the importance in giving a strong commitment and setting a positive example to the community. Whether at St. Joe's, the Minneapolis Veterans Home, or other volunteer connections, he shows where his heart is on every visit.

"It means a lot to us," says Kluwe. "It is our way to help give back to the community. They come out and support us every game. They are the ones who provide our paychecks. It is the very least we can do to come out and help these kids out. A lot of them have had a rough time in life, and whatever we can do to help them out, it makes us feel better. You can see their eyes light up when they see us. To them, it's the guys they see on television all the time. We are known as the Vikings. If we can come in and make them happy, it's all worth it. Staff told us if we can make just one of these kids smile so they aren't thinking about their personal situation, it makes it all worthwhile."

When it comes to community commitment, giving back, and the importance of it all, Tony Richardson stands tall and strong. Richardson, a tough, bruising blocking back who has endured 12 seasons in the NFL, is as dedicated and committed to working with youth as he is on the gridiron.

The Minnesota Vikings were fortunate to gain Richardson's athletic abilities when they obtained him this past year from the Kansas City Chiefs and have benefited from his work both on and off the field.

Richardson is committed to educating young people. He has obtained a bachelor's degree and an MBA and knows the importance of education. Tony Richardson is a dedicated and solid example of a quality person. He is admired and praised for his off-field accomplishments.

"I would not be in the position I am in without education," says Richardson. "I remember when I was in the third grade and a teacher would ask a question, and I would slide down in my chair not knowing the answer."

"It's easy to write a check to someone, but it is more important to give personally. I sometimes get more out of it than the kids. My parents really stressed education, and some kids don't have that. It puts my focus on what is more important. It makes you realize the game is not so big. It keeps things in the right perspective when you get back to work."

Tony Richardson is actively involved in the community through the Boys and Girls Club and Special Olympics. But where the athlete really excels with children is in the classroom. He has a student "Dictionary Project" in which he visits grade schools and hands out dictionaries to kids. Giving the dictionary to each child is only a small part of the program. It is the interaction he has with youngsters during the program that puts his special imprint on it.

Richardson started the program when he was with the Kansas City Chiefs and has since donated over 45,000 dictionaries to students. In 2006, Tony donated over 6,000 dictionaries to every third grade student in the St. Paul and Minneapolis Public Schools.

Richardson speaks to the classes about the importance of education. He has the children look up words in the dictionary, discusses the meaning of those words with them, and teaches them how they can be used in daily conversation. He has a knack of making the learning experience wonderful for the youngsters.

On the inside of each personal dictionary is a place for the child's name and a sticker that reads, "RICH 49 in Spirit FOUNDATION NFL Charities est. 1973. Reaching out to help Minnesota's Youth. Tony Richardson of the Minnesota Vikings presents this dictionary to you on behalf of THE DIC-TION-AR-Y PROJECT."

It is not just the idea behind the project and the athlete's school visits that stand out in the program. It is Tony Richardson's passion, dedication, and commitment to every child that makes the community connection such a major success.

On September 12, 2006, Tony Richardson went to Wenonah Community School with his Dictionary Project and met with its third graders. During the program, the athlete had every student write his or her name in a personal dictionary, so each could take pride in owning the great educational tool. As Richardson participated with the students, his eyes gleamed, and it was obvious his heart was proud.

"The Dictionary Project" is a national non-profit organization. Its goal is to assist students in becoming good writers, creative thinkers, and active readers all by use of the dictionary. The program is designed to build a foundation for education. "It gives the children another tool to be successful in life," says Richardson. "It helps them to set their goals high and have a back-up plan. You can never learn enough."

Joan Hultman, principal of Wenonah Community School, speaks highly of Richardson's program. She tells of his "knowledge and enthusiasm" and says that teachers went away in "awe" after the program. What made the program a success was certainly the concept, but it was Richardson who put real quality into the work and made it an incredible experience for everyone present.

The Minnesota Vikings were successful in receiving a great athlete when Tony Richardson joined the team. From the community standpoint, however, it is clear they also obtained a wonderful and giving person. He is a great representative of the Minnesota Vikings and a valuable personality to the community connection.

In addition to Richardson's Dictionary Project, the Vikings have also attended Wenonah Community School for a few other events. In October of 2006, Kenechi Udeze and Jason Glenn came to the school in recognition of NFL Hispanic Heritage month to award students with tickets to the Vikings' game against the Detroit Lions.

This program recognized the winners of a diversity essay contest and allowed for those students to read their winning essays in front of others at the school.

The warmth shown by Kenechi and Glenn was evident as they interacted with students in the auditorium. On their day off in the middle of the season, these two first-class individuals committed time to be involved in a valuable learning experience. The day was full of joy and the program was wonderful. Both the community and Minnesota Vikings were winners again.

Joan Hultman has been in the first row to witness many of the events put on by the Vikings for the children in her school. She has been very impressed with the team's work. "The Vikings are vitally engaged in education and they say, 'Here is something for you,'" explains Hultman. "They extend into the community."

She continues, stating, "The reality of a team taking its time to come and interact with the kids is incredible. They really look up to the players who come into the school and say, 'Wow, they are special!'"

In anticipation of a future visit, one of the children said, "I think I saw one of the Vikings here today!" Sadly, the little one was reminded that the event was scheduled for a different day. But the reality is clear what something like this means to the students. They look for their Vikings even when they aren't scheduled to be there. "To give their valuable time is the greatest gift they can give," says Hultman.

So what were you doing on June 8, 2006?

It was a beautiful day in the Twin Cities. The sun was bright and warm. Maybe you went golfing or perhaps to the beach. Maybe you took a walk or a run, or just enjoyed the wonderful weather.

Whatever it was that you did on this day, the Vikings did something different. They didn't have practice, hold a meeting, or watch film. On this day, the Minnesota Vikings' team, staff, and coaches helped to construct a playground at Wenonah Community School in Minneapolis. Over 100 players and staff representing the

Vikings and more than 250 volunteers joined forces to build a new and safe playground at the school.

The Vikings and the Toro Company partnered on its construction, which was a great success. The two organizations have worked together on projects like this for the past four years and have already committed to another this summer.

Judson Tharin, senior community relations specialist for the Toro Company, truly recognizes the Vikings' role in giving back to the community. "The Vikings committed $30,000 dollars to the project and the entire organization to assist in the building of the playground," says Judson. And that wasn't all. The team also spent a day designing and a day preparing for the project.

"It was great to see the Vikings as people just like us," says Tharin. "To see the five buses full of Vikings pull up in front of the school was impressive. Childress blew his whistle and they all gathered and listened. He really took charge of the situation."

Tharin thinks a great deal of Brad Childress' commitment as Vikings head coach. "There is no question he is genuine about this type of endeavor. He wants to give back to the community. It is very important to him," she says with great regard for the Vikings' leader.

In addition to working on the playground's construction, many of the players also participated in various activities with students in the classroom. On this day, that child who previously said, "I think I saw one of the Vikings here today" would have been correct to comment, "I think I saw about 100 Vikings at the school today!"

Community events, a way of giving back to those in need, have always been very important to the Minnesota Vikings. In fact, the organization has been one of the NFL's leaders in outreach. And meeting these expectations every week during the season is the team's director of community relations, Brad Madson.

Many organizations are satisfied when an individual in a position of responsibility handles the ultimate duties of that position in a competent and professional manner. But some positions in the workplace may, to some extent, go unnoticed. Madson puts the

Vikings in the forefront through their connection to the area. His work is exceptional in honoring the team's commitment to others.

As the director of community relations with the Minnesota Vikings, Brad Madson has mastered this responsibility in exemplary fashion. Not only does he connect the Vikings players and alumni to the community, but he connects them in a passionate, heartfelt manner.

When looking at the duties and responsibilities that go with any employment position, it is always in an organization's best interest to find an individual whose personality matches the job. And if there was ever a "match made in heaven," this is it.

This isn't a job, a salary, a place of employment, or a responsibility for Brad Madson; it is a calling. He is a devoted, committed, hard-working person who has taken on his role with the Vikings and performed it in a manner worthy of the highest esteem. He does the job with an internal commitment and strives for excellence.

Much talk has circulated through the memorable years of this storied franchise regarding the Vikings' failure to win a Super Bowl. Little commentary is wasted on the fact that the Vikings have participated in four of them. With respect to giving back in life, however, Brad Madson and the Minnesota Vikings play a Super Bowl every Tuesday. And with the assistance of the players, the partnership agencies, and the recipients of their goodwill, a lifetime of victory occurs on a regular basis. Every single week that the Minnesota Vikings and Brad Madson are out in the community, the Vikings WIN THE SUPER BOWL!

Matt Birk, Vikings All-Pro center, throws a pass to a fourth grader from Eastern Heights Elementary School in St. Paul. The young boy catches the football, beaming with excitement. He has run out for the pass a little differently than the other members of his class. This little boy is in a wheelchair.

Earlier in the day, he had smiled at Christine Fox, a 20-year employee of the school district, while sitting at a table in the Vikings' lunchroom. Fox responded to the little boy in a gleeful manner, saying, "Why, that's the first time I have seen you smile in a long time!" Even though the day had barely begun, the Vikings' visit could have successfully ended at that moment. The little boy found something to smile about that day and now wears his Vikings jacket to school year-round.

It was a special day for Mr. Chuck Worthington's class from Eastern Heights Elementary School. On December 12, 2006, Birk hosted a pizza party and play day for the elementary students because they had won the Gridiron Geography contest set up by the Vikings/*Star Tribune* Geography Program. Eastern Heights was chosen for the award through a drawing of the classrooms that had participated in the program. During the event, Matt Birk was also named Vikings' Man of the Year for the fifth consecutive year.

Kathleen Farrell, educational service manager for the *Minneapolis Star Tribune*, indicated that Matt Birk has been involved in the youth education program for several years. "It gives the children great experience to be able to relate to a player for the Minnesota Vikings," says Farrell. "The program is designed as a geography contest to bring the students to the newspaper to find the contest answers. The Vikings are so accommodating and Brad Madson is so wonderful with the children."

Farrell speaks proudly about the program and highly of Matt Birk. "He is so highly educated, such a gentleman, and relates so well to the kids. He is such a strong role model for the program," she says.

Running, conditioning exercises, and catching passes were all in store for the youngsters who spent their day at Winter Park. Matt Birk and Brad Madson, with assistance from player development assistant Isaiah Harris, worked hard to make the event a success and had fun in the process. The Vikings' personnel seemed to get almost as much out of the day as the children.

"It was a great day for the kids," says the students' teacher, Chuck Worthington. "They never get an opportunity to do something like this. The kids took the pictures we took and made a giant poster and

Center Matt Birk receives "Viking Man of the Year" for the fifth consecutive time for his many efforts within the community.

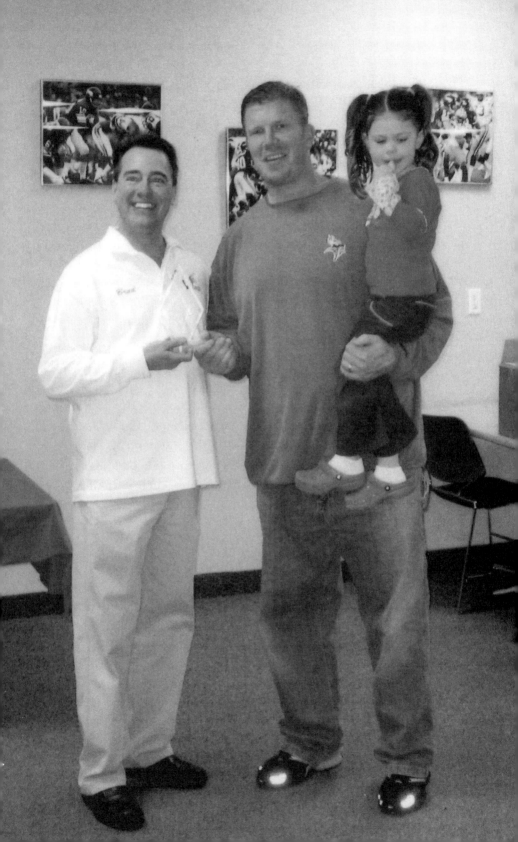

have them hanging on the wall. They talked about it for a week straight."

Worthington continues to praise every aspect of the event, especially Matt Birk. "The kids said how big he was. His size and his strength were amazing. It was great how he held up the blocking pad and had the kids hit it and threw passes to all the kids."

Matt Birk, Vikings leader on the field and in the community, is a role model for youth. In winning Man of the Year recognition for the fifth time, Birk has continued to demonstrate his commitment to the community.

Since becoming a part of the Minnesota Vikings in 1998, he has been devoted to charity work, becoming a community icon. He supports all of his teammates' efforts and has graciously formed his own HIKE Foundation, which stands for Hope, Inspiration, Knowledge and Education.

The HIKE Foundation was established by the Vikings' Pro Bowl center "to provide at-risk Twin Cities children with the educational opportunities needed to excel in the classroom and in life. The Foundation impacts the lives of at-risk children by providing interactive programs and resources needed to guide a child through the key educational transitions between elementary, middle, high school, and college."

Birk is also the team spokesman for the United Way, and has given of his time with many local charities by making many school and hospital visits.

As the grade school youngsters prepared to retrieve passes at Winter Park, Birk explained the end zone's significance. He noted to the kids how large of an area it was, paused for a moment, and quietly said, "As large as it is, you would think we would get in there more often." Then the fun began.

What made the little boy's success even more joyous was the fact that he had retrieved Birk's pass in the end zone of the indoor football field at the Minnesota Vikings' practice facility. Observing this young boy's wonderful feat was certainly very special. He had endured several rough months after all the bones in his legs had to be broken for surgeries that will hopefully allow him to walk again someday.

As the Vikings' event took place, however, one couldn't be too sure which was more significant, the sparkle in this boy's eyes or the enthusiasm across Brad Madson's face. If an outsider didn't know the circumstances, he might have guessed that Madson had caught a pass in front of thousands at the Super Bowl. Instead, he was the wheelchair's driver and the little boy was the receiver.

The public generally believes that winning every Sunday is what professional football is all about. Finishing first in the division, succeeding in the playoffs, and making the trip to the Super Bowl are all that matter when it comes to the Minnesota Vikings football team.

Calling the right play, attacking the defense, and stopping the opponent's offense are in every NFL team's job description. When an individual steps out of his uniform and draws attention by doing something inappropriate, his actions may have more ramifications than anything done on the playing field. What is important in life takes a back seat to everything else and is soon forgotten.

Winter Park and the Vikings have a strong commitment to assisting community agencies and people in need, and they do it more than most will ever know. Maybe these stories aren't as good as a loss on Sunday or a player's trouble off the field, and that's a shame, because this organization has a strong commitment to help others and has demonstrated the effort for many years.

On Tuesday, December 12, 2006, the Vikings won a big game at Winter Park. They won it with a class of grade school kids who had the opportunity to meet Matt Birk, Vikings Pro Bowl center. They got to run with him, catch passes from him, and eat pizza with him. It was a special day—a day of giving and a day of great reward. And for one little boy in a wheelchair, it can all be summed up by a rare grin.

Chad Knapp can make anyone smile. His refreshing and positive outlook is contagious. Chad has cerebral palsy. He is 13, has had six surgeries, and is now walking and doing well.

Brad Madson has a special, heartfelt connection with Chad and his family. It started some years back with a touchdown pass thrown to former Viking Randy Moss on January 3, 2000. Moss, as he had done so many times after a catch, delivered the ball to Chad, who was sitting in his wheelchair near the end zone. The act began a great relationship with the Minnesota Vikings.

Chad is a wonderful little boy with a huge heart who plans to someday be a football coach. He had a great mentor this year, when Vikings' head coach Brad Childress spent time with him at Winter Park.

"This is a side of Brad Childress not seen by many," says Chad's mother, Becky Lee. Through arrangements by community relations director Brad Madson, Chad and his mom attended a Vikings practice session, met with the players, and spoke privately with Coach Childress.

"What type of protection are you going to use on this play?" is just one of the many questions the coach posed as the two talked football. Chad attends the Vikings' training camp at Mankato every July and participates in the Vikings' events at the Shriners Hospital in Minneapolis. He has attended other Vikings practices through the years as well.

On one occasion, former Viking Cris Carter took Chad out on the field so the future coach could have a closer look. Carter found this little boy to be something extraordinary, and made the child's mom cry when he said, "God gave you a special child. You are very lucky."

When observing Chad Knapp, it is easy to realize the really lucky ones are those who have had the opportunity to associate with him. He brings meaning to life and helps others truly understand what is important. He puts everything in its proper perspective.

"Chad is probably the biggest football fan you will ever find," says his mom. "He will never play the game—he can't play the

Aspiring coach Chad Knapp (right) smiles alongside guard Steve Hutchinson at the Shriners Hospital.

game—so he will be a coach. When players and former players like Cris Carter, Ed McDaniel, John Randle, Jim Kleinsasser, Daunte Culpepper, and Steve Hutchinson, and coaches like Brad Childress, Mike Tice, Denny Green, and others tell Chad, 'This is what you have to do to be a coach. You are on the right track,' it means so much to him."

Chad has been connected to the Shriners Hospital for many years and now visits annually for checkups. He is always around when the Vikings pay a visit. And this wonderful story all began just a few years ago, when Vikings wide receiver Randy Moss presented a football to Chad. It was the beginning of an everlasting bond between a little boy and his Vikings.

This year, Steve Hutchinson, Vikings All-Pro offensive guard, made a visit of his own undertaking to the Shriners Hospital to donate Thanksgiving turkeys to each family currently being served at the hospital. It was a glorious experience for the children in attendance and the families present. Hutchinson signed autographs, had pictures taken with the children and the parents, and visited hospital rooms.

It was easily recognized that this was not an obligation for Steve Hutchinson. This was not an individual who'd say, "I'll take a few minutes for the less fortunate and be done with it." This was a man who devoted himself for several hours of the day to enrich the lives of others.

All one had to do was look at the deep commitment in his eyes to tell the visit may have meant more to Steve Hutchinson than anyone he came in contact with on this special day.

Aimee Olson is a recreation and child life specialist at the Shriners Hospital. She relays the importance of a special day like November 21, 2006, by explaining, "The kids are excited about this kind of event ahead of time. They are all saying, 'The Vikings are coming tomorrow!' We have some children who just came back to Shriners just to see the Vikings. These kids can't play physically, so this type of thing brings some normalcy to their lives."

"This was a great day," says Olson. "One of the children could not come down to the room where the event was held, so Steve Hutchinson went to the child's room. It brought the child's mom to tears.

"When something like this occurs, it makes the kids realize the abilities they do have and causes them to have a new frame of mind. They are able to set new goals and realize there is nothing they can't do. It makes them believe that they should never let anyone tell them that they cannot succeed."

The Shriners Hospitals are wonderful facilities, providing pediatric health care for children at no charge to the patients' families. They are continually striving to provide compassionate hospital and medical care to children with orthopedic disabilities or burn damage. They are at the forefront of medical research and treatment in burn, orthopedic, and spinal cord injuries. They have provided medical services to over 770,000 patients.

Ruth Brinkman's daughter, Mary, has scoliosis and has been connected to the great work done by the Shriners Hospital. She was in attendance the day Steve Hutchinson spent time at the hospital.

"It meant a lot to us," says Brinkman. "It shows that they care about other things than just what happens on the field. It is great they take time out of their schedule to visit the children. We are not really into football that much, but it meant a lot to see a player in person."

Brinkman was impressed at Hutchinson's compassion and warmth for the hospital kids. "He did a great outreach job and showed us there was more to his life than football. We see or hear about the players on the radio or television, and to see them in person was special."

"This wasn't even a planned community outing," says Brad Madson, community relations director. "Steve called me and said he wanted to go to the hospital, give away turkeys for Thanksgiving, and visit the children." Hutchinson's initiative made the day that much more meaningful.

In addition to the Shriners Hospital, the state of Minnesota has also been fortunate to be the resident home of the Courage St. Croix Center, a nonprofit rehabilitation and resource center for those with disabilities. Since 1928, the Center has been creating abilities, possibilities, and independence for people of all ages with disabilities. It serves those with brain and spinal cord injuries, neurological conditions, chronic pain, and congenital difficulties.

The program involves a continuum of services that includes outpatient rehabilitation, transitional programming, pain management services, wellness and fitness programs, vocational services, and provides many other opportunities to assist those with physical challenges.

A wonderful, genuine operation with incredible staff, the Courage Center is a United Way agency that has worked on many occasions with the Minnesota Vikings to make life better for those with disability issues.

Sharon Van Winkle is one of those dedicated and committed staff members who has seen the Vikings assist with many of the Center's programming needs. "The Minnesota Vikings recognize when there is a community need," says Van Winkle. "And when they give their recognition, it means the world to those receiving it. They have assisted us through player appearances for special events and have financially helped us through the United Way and the Viking Children's Fund.

"Vikings center Matt Birk has appeared at events to assist the Courage Center. He once took a Saturday of his own time to appear at our annual banquet to speak, answer questions, and to sign autographs," says Van Winkle. "The kids who heard Matt Birk speak were awestruck. And the kids responded so well to him that Matt said, 'I have never heard such adult questions from a group of kids before.'"

Van Winkle responds to Birk's comment by saying that children with disabilities are very "savvy." As Van Winkle explains, "The challenging experiences in their lives make them wiser than their years."

All one has to do is hear the excitement and passion in the voice of Peter Polga, the director of the Courage St. Croix Center, to realize the greatness of this organization and the commitment the Center has to helping those with physical disabilities. Not only does Polga proudly speak about the Courage Center's programs and its deep commitment to helping others, but he also expresses his appreciation and affection for Vikings Pro Bowl center Matt Birk. Polga lived across the street from Birk as the athlete grew up.

The Vikings have left a great mark with the Courage Center for over 25 years. "People like Matt Birk, former Viking Stu Voigt, and many others are always willing to help us," says a proud Sharon Van Winkle. "They are able to find a way to solidify in the brains of the children that they, too, are important."

Several past Vikings players continue to participate in community outreach. On Sunday afternoons in the fall, he wore No. 88 and was one of the most dominating defensive players to ever play the game. He was Alan Page, and the Viking faithful marveled at what this man was able to accomplish on the football field. However, those achievements are of little importance next to what he's done off it.

Justice Alan Page, a member of the Minnesota Supreme Court, doesn't talk much about football, but will speak with passion when referring to the Page Education Foundation and what it has meant to underprivileged children in aiding their education.

In 2005, Justice Page received the Distinguished American Award from the National Football Foundation and College Hall of Fame: "Presented on special occasions when a truly deserving individual emerges, the award honors someone who has applied the character-building attributes learned from amateur sport in their business and personal life, exhibiting superior leadership qualities in education, amateur athletics, business, and in the community. Alan becomes the award's 34th recipient, joining a list that includes Vince Lombardi, Bob Hope, Jimmy Stewart, Pete Rozelle, and Tom Osborne."

Justice Thurgood Marshall, former member of the United States Supreme Court, says, "None of us has gotten where we are by pulling ourselves up by our bootstraps. We got here because somebody bent down and helped us." The Alan Page Education Foundation, established in 1988, does exactly that.

The most mentionable attribute of this incredible foundation is the structure in which it operates and strives. It develops "Page Scholars" and assists each with their educational pursuits. However, additionally and most importantly, it provides resources through which the scholars assist others in their educations. For example, in 2005, 565 Page Scholars will reach 6,500 children of color as they give back to the community, serving as role models, tutors, and mentors to younger students.

It is an incredible opportunity for the youngsters of color to be aided in their educational dreams while also affording the opportunity to others as part of their Page Scholar responsibilities. With a foundation built on helping others, this program is a positive approach to education.

Through financial contributions and fundraisers, the educational opportunities become a reality, and through volunteers, those not receiving scholarships are assisted as well. It is an infectious process and highly contagious. As each scholar is identified, recognized, and honored, many more students will be mentored and assisted with their educational opportunities.

Alycia Woolcock is an example of this tremendous educational work in progress. As the Page Education Foundation reports, "As a student, Alycia is curious, diligent, and enthusiastic. And, as a volunteer working with children, she earns extra high marks from both her supervisor and from youngsters at the Minneapolis American Indian Center, where she tutors kids ages 10 to 14. 'Setting a good example for kids is rewarding on many levels. I'm proud of my students, and that sense of pride, plus the knowledge that I'm making a difference, inspires me.'"

This inspirational message is a quick and miniscule look at what is important for today's youth. Such programs, developed and strongly believed in by former Minnesota Vikings players like Alan Page, are deserving of recognition and worthy of the highest regard. It is important for the community to take a close look at programs like this, understand their significance, and reach out to assist. With more volunteers, the Page Education Foundation will be able to enhance its efforts to achieve even greater results.

The Minnesota Vikings' commitment to the community is demonstrated through such highly committed individuals as former Viking Justice Alan Page, Pro Football Hall of Famer, Ring of Honor Member, and outstanding citizen.

Page came from a family where education was very important, and he realized early in his life it was the key to success. In the 1950s to 1960, he saw that people idolized athletes—often in discriminatory ways. Too much attention was focused on athletics and not education, and Page set out to change that. He strongly believes that people have a responsibility to help others and that education is a solution to many problems. While he has much more to accomplish, Alan Page has made an incredible impact on society.

Other former Vikings also understand the necessity of giving back to the community and do it on a regular basis in meaningful ways. Twin Cities local radio personality Mike Morris played for the Vikings for nine of his 13 years in the NFL, from 1991 to 1999. Morris really gets what life is all about. For the past seven years, he has worked diligently through many fundraising events to raise money for Spinal Muscular Atrophy, or SMA.

"It all started when some of my children's school friends had the disease," says Morris. "It was simply the time to get up and do something! I have been very fortunate in my life and I feel a responsibility to give back to those less fortunate.

"Everyone needs a shot at life. I got that and others are deserving of it also. We must find a way in our lives to help others. These situations are real—real life-and-death situations."

With the help of many others in his commitment to SMA, Morris has raised one million dollars to assist in the fighting of this horrific disease. His goal to continue on with the mission is unstoppable and deserving of high praise. But he doesn't do it for the recognition; he does it because it is the right thing to do.

Mike Morris appreciates his past with the Minnesota Vikings and his association with other great players who have learned the importance of their community contributions. "People like Randall McDaniel, Tim Irwin, Steve Jordan, and many others did all they could do to keep their bodies together every week of the season, yet they always found the time to give back to the community. They did it because they wanted to, not because they had to," says Morris proudly.

Morris speaks passionately of the opportunity to make a difference in the lives of others. And he has a message to the fans, the Vikings organization, the community, and all those who have supported him along the way. It is a deep, heartfelt "THANK YOU."

Former running back Oscar Reed speaks with the same desire as Mike Morris when referencing the importance of giving one's self to aid and assist those in need. Reed played for the Vikings for seven years from 1968 to 1974. The bone-crushing ball carrier brings his commitment to schools and the community to assist young people in need of positive role models. Reed has been involved in helping kids for many years and understands the importance of his work in the Twin Cities. "I raised my children here," says Reed. "This is a great area."

Both Mike Morris and Oscar Reed appreciate what the area has done for them. When asked to speak to the Viking organization, the fans, and the community, Oscar Reed's reply, like that of Mike Morris', is a deeply positive "THANK YOU."

Former and current players alike continue to make the Minnesota community proud. As youngsters ran up and down a gymnasium floor on November 28, 2006, Spencer Johnson and Alex Guerrero of the Minnesota Vikings interacted with each of them. This wasn't a real football drill, where the banging of heads can make one's teeth chatter or develop headaches in those merely watching. This was the Academic Training Camp conducted at Monroe Community School by the Minnesota Vikings on one of their many

"Community Tuesdays," where giving back is of the utmost of importance.

The training camp was part of a program called A.C.E.S., which stands for Athletes Committed to Educating Students, and its goal was not only for children to have fun with Vikings players, but also learn in the process. Math and football, combined with a good time, made a great learning experience for each of the participants.

Penny Reynen is the executive director of A.C.E.S. She says it is the best job she has ever had. Her gratitude toward the Minnesota Vikings and the assistance they give to the kids and program is heartfelt.

"The players are phenomenal with the kids," says Reynen. "They give so much to the community. 'When are they coming back?' is the remark we hear from the children after the Vikings leave after the event."

Reynen is committed to the program and speaks of its enhancement when the players are involved. "These players and the team don't have to do this. They do it because it is the right thing to do. Some of these kids are not easy to engage in things, and the players always talk to them in respectful ways. It sends the message to stay in school," she says.

All any individual has to do is watch great people like Spencer Johnson and Alex Guerrero, who also happen to be great athletes, working with the kids on football drills and math problems to understand the real importance of what they do in the community with their free time.

The event is a success for the program and its goals. It is also a success for the players and kids. All one has to do is look at the children's faces. Having a good time, learning, and being around their heroes are things they will never forget.

Like Spencer Johnson, Alex Guerrero is dedicated to the community and its youth. Both love what they do in the area and are proud of it. And Guerrero's infectious smile also lights up the room. He came to the Vikings midway through the 2006 season after having been with several other teams earlier in the year. His community commitment is second to none. "I was raised to be a person to give back to others," says Guerrero. "My family told me to never take for granted what we have."

Outreach is never an obligation for Guerrero, but always something he wants to do. "At Boise State, I won the Humanitarian Award," Guerrero proudly states. "I worked more than 50 hours past my community commitment."

During the A.C.E.S. Academic Training Camp, Guerrero gave back to the community at Monroe Community School, and on December 12, 2006, he was involved in the Shop with a Viking program through the Vikings' player partnership with Dick's Sporting Goods. There is no doubt he enjoyed the day and loved spending time with the kids.

The Vikings players were scheduled to spend $100 gift cards, courtesy of Dick's Sporting Goods, with approximately 30 children from the Boys and Girls Clubs of the Twin Cities. In addition, the players donated two tickets to each youngster for the Vikings/New York Jets game on December 17, 2006.

Guerrero's face lit up when talking about the event. "One of the children wanted the $100 to use as an investment," he laughed. "And another wanted to use the money to buy presents for his family for Christmas."

Alex Guerrero called this experience "the best!" It was a great day for the Vikings players who took part, and a special moment for each of the children involved. "We feel like maybe we can change a couple of these kids' lives," says Guerrero. Even the opportunity to do so makes it all worthwhile.

When visiting children who are hospitalized with serious illnesses, players may not be able to change lives long term. However, just affecting a child for one moment makes the effort so very important. When the Minnesota Vikings take the opportunity to do this, the rewards are incredible.

On September 26, 2006, Mike Rosenthal, Jason Carter, Chad Greenway, Marcus Johnson, Cullen Loeffler, Donald Penn, Ross Kolodziej, Tony Richardson, Khreem Smith, and Jason Whittle visited the University of Minnesota Children's Hospital, Fairview in Minneapolis.

The visit was made in conjunction with the Viking Children's Fund. Since its inception in 1978, the VCF has donated more than four million dollars to the University of Minnesota Department of Pediatrics to support research in fighting childhood diseases.

Rosenthal, who came to the Vikings from the New York Giants in 2003, has been a regular in visiting hospitals and a true, inspirational leader in this regard. He and others feel that it is not an obligation on their day off, but rather an important way to give back to the community. Taking the time to closely look at each child's expression makes the event worth every minute of the players' commitment and provides support for those in such grave need.

Former Viking Ross Kolodziej says, "We get more out of the visits than the kids do. If we can help out a family or an individual in a tough situation, it makes it all worth it. We are very blessed, and it is part of our responsibility to do this."

A longtime relationship exists among the University of Minnesota Children's Hospital, Fairview, the Minnesota Vikings, and the Children's Fund. As a child life specialist, Jason Albrecht has been a part of this connection for the past 12 years. He works with the children and families as they enter into and remain in an atmosphere few are familiar with. Grave sicknesses and, at times, death are not a part of the general public's world, yet Albrecht deals with them every day.

"The children here are the sickest of the sick in the region," say Albrecht. Many of the kids cannot leave their rooms, and it means so much when the players come to see them.

Albrecht says the children's responses are incredible. "These guys came to my room to see me!" he often hears them say. "It makes them feel so special."

Albrecht, whose responsibilities include hosting and giving the players tours when they visit the children's hospital, generally has a short talk with all visiting Vikings, asking them to look past the tubes, scars, and medical equipment to relate directly to the children.

Former Vikings tackle Mike Rosenthal (left) and running back Wendell Mathis visit a child at the University of Minnesota Children's Hospital, Fairview.

It can sometimes be a tough task to accomplish, but is always done so well by the players.

"I have never seen a Vikings player who was not able to accomplish the goal put before them—to look past the equipment and to the child," says Albrecht. "The Minnesota Vikings players have quickly recognized their power to do good and really snap into a nurturing-type role."

Although he is now with the Miami Dolphins, Mike Rosenthal was a major part of the visits and is recognized for the outstanding commitment he made to those children in such dire need of his presence.

"Former Vikings kicker Gary Anderson also made a significant impact on the children," says Albrecht. "He approached the visits like a dad, and truly made the kids feel like the visit was all about them."

Anderson, one of the greatest kickers in NFL history, seems to be most remembered for his missed field goal against the Atlanta Falcons in 1998, which knocked the Vikings out of the playoffs. It is probably fair to say that Gary Anderson kicked a lot more important field goals during his incredible visits to the University of Minnesota Children's Hospital, Fairview. And he made every one of them— right through the uprights in life.

Jason Albrecht speaks of the way the children relate to their heroes when the players' visits follow a Viking loss. The tables sometimes turn at these times as the children try to provide comfort for the players. "You're okay. You did a good job, it's okay," they may say to their Sunday warriors. "Many a player has looked for the Kleenex box on those visits," recalls Albrecht.

The children's preparations prior to the visits are amazing and tug at the heartstrings. "Some kids are not into sports at all, but some write home and have their parents send them a jersey to wear from their hometown to show it off."

Others have had their parents take a several-hour drive to retrieve their favorite jerseys to wear when the Vikings visit. Albrecht says most wear as much purple as possible, including the parents, who also want the Vikings to know that they support the Purple.

As a seven-year-old, Jason Albrecht himself was hospitalized with cancer. The Minnesota Vikings paid him a visit. Now 37 years old, he helps bring the athletes to others in need. It is his life's mission and a job he feels fortunate to have. The Vikings' visit was a memorable experience for Albrecht. Thirty years later, the Purple are still visiting hospitals.

About the children and the impact of the Vikings' work, Jason says, "These children and their families enter every day trying to find ways to make their lives better." No doubt "better" is an ingredient that arrives when the Minnesota Vikings come to the children's hospital.

The Vikings' opportunities at hospitals, schools, and other places within the community have differed greatly from one another. One event at Black Hawk Middle School in Eagan, Minnesota, was quite unusual. In this program, which took place on October 24, 2006, the Vikings worked with the NFL and the American Heart Association to fight childhood obesity.

Steve Hutchinson, the Vikings' All-Pro guard, was present to help kids supervise and participate in exercises and other activities. The program, WHAT MOVES U, encourages youth to become physically active. Hutchinson showed them many ways to do this and how to keep things up on a regular basis.

As part of the physical fitness campaign, every middle school in Minnesota is provided with a curriculum activity kit, created by teachers for teachers and personalized by the Vikings. The kits are provided at no charge, courtesy of the Minnesota Vikings, the NFL, and the American Heart Association. The program's design brings physical activity to the classroom and into typical classes that normally do not include it, such as math and English.

Barbara Ducharme, marketing director for the American Heart Association, helped coordinate the school event and was very pleased with the outcome. She feels strongly that combining efforts with the Vikings has a significant impact.

"It gives the program visibility for what we are trying to do and entry into the community," says Barbara. "Steve Hutchinson did a great job! He was highly recommended by the Vikings and he was so good at working with the kids."

Hutchinson gave great encouragement to sixth and seventh grade students as he ran drills and promoted good health. He also demonstrated various activities, including a spelling relay where students ran to pick up letter cards in order to spell out words.

Participation from the Vikings' great offensive guard may have been enough. In fact, his presence may have been all that was needed to make the program successful. But to watch Steve Hutchinson contribute was incredible. He connected with his heart and his spirit, ran drills with emotion and inspiration, and made the program a booming victory in every respect.

Wendell Mathis (No. 34) and Tarvaris Jackson (No. 7) prepare a Thanksgiving meal at the Salvation Army Harbor Light Center.

Hutchinson is another Minnesota Viking who gives as much to others off the field as he ever gives on it. He is an inspirational human being who really understands what is important in life.

Vikings quarterbacks Brooks Bollinger and Tarvaris Jackson also understand the need for outreach. If one were to have walked back into the kitchen of the Salvation Harbor Light Center in downtown Minneapolis on November 21, 2006, he or she would not have seen Bollinger and Jackson throwing footballs around the room. Rather, he would have seen them preparing Thanksgiving meals for those in need.

Spencer Johnson, Khreem Smith, Darrion Scott, and Dru-Ann Childress joined Bollinger and Jackson in their volunteer efforts toward a long tradition between the Vikings and The Salvation Army. It was an inspirational afternoon full of giving and interacting, something few football fans ever have the opportunity to witness.

Since Zygi Wilf became an owner of the Minnesota Vikings, he has strongly supported the concept of giving back to the community. Following up on the thoughts of Bud Grant and teams from the '60s, this process has been of longstanding importance to the Vikings and their surrounding areas as the community connection lives on.

Zygi Wilf demonstrated his commitment on October 31, 2006. On a bitter, cold day, along with the NFL, Project for Pride in Living, and the Twin Cities Local Initiatives Support Corporation, players Marcus Johnson and Jim Kleinsasser joined Wilf at Parade Stadium in Minneapolis, Minnesota, to donate $200,000 dollars to assist with the Minneapolis Park and Recreation Board's Parade Stadium refurbishment. After the award presentation, a youth fun skills competition took place in which Kleinsasser and Johnson worked with young football teams in attendance.

The project design is to help young players across the country enjoy the game of football. Parade Stadium has been a major part of the community for many years. The NFL's Community Football Field Program is part of the NFL Charities Youth Football Fund, a multimillion-dollar effort of the NFL and its individual franchises—such as the Vikings—in partnership with the NFL Players Association, which ensures that kids nationwide have the opportunity to benefit from football.

Other faces within the Vikings organization also commit to various causes. Rob Brzezinski, vice president of football operations for the Purple, has a couple other great passions in his life in addition to the Vikings—both his family and the personal role they have taken in adoption. On November 7, 2006, at the Vikings' headquarters in Winter Park, Brzezinski and his wife, Leah, as well as their children, Ki and Grace, hosted a family fun event to support adoptions.

The event included interactive games, face painting, complex tours, snacks, and time for autographs. Many players also participated in the evening, working with youngsters on the team's practice field. Vikings in attendance were Richard Angulo, Jason Carter, E.J.

Henderson, Bethel Johnson, and Ben Leber. The proceeds from the event went to the Children's Home Society and Family Services of the Twin Cities.

"We always felt in our heart we wanted to adopt children," says Brzezinski. "It is an awesome experience for parents to experience."

The family had a common goal in mind for the fundraiser. Not only did the event raise money, but it also created awareness, helping people to understand the importance of adoption. "Getting someone to 'scratch their heads' and say, 'We need to look into this' is a primary goal of the event as well," explains Brzezinski.

Brzezinski sits in a beautiful office overlooking Winter Park's practice field and interacts daily with great athletes. He is involved in multimillion-dollar football contracts and has enjoyed a great reputation for his work throughout the NFL. Yet, when it comes down to the important things in his life, Brzezinski sums it up in a simple statement: "Nothing is more important to me than my wife and my children."

While the Brzezinski family has met success with fundraisers of its own, other individuals show their commitment to community through other organizations. Kristine Huson, public relations manager for the Children's Home Society and Family Services, speaks passionately about professional athletes and others who call the agency willing to help without calling public attention to themselves. Their community work, as experienced through the Children's Home Society and Family Services, is most rewarding.

"The role that they play in planting a message in a child's mind is something that will never be forgotten," says Huson. "I have always been very impressed at the age of the players and how they negotiate through something they have no experience with. They truly learn and understand the big picture, and they do so well in the process."

Helping out at clothing drives, giving blood, hosting non-perishable food drives, collecting Toys for Tots, assisting underprivileged youngsters in getting their eyes tested for glasses, and aiding in other events and fundraisers have all been part of the Vikings' commitment to the community for many decades.

The *Minnesota Vikings Community Report* speaks of its history in helping Minnesota children: "There have been many changes on and off the field for the Minnesota Vikings since the team's inception, but the organization's strong commitment to kids has always remained the same."

The Viking Children's Fund, or VCF, was created in 1978 and has donated $7.35 million back to the community. The VCF was established to help children in need and as a means for Vikings players, coaches, cheerleaders, staff, and their families to focus on community support. The VCF distributes grants to health, education, and family services organizations benefiting children.

This year, the VCF provided more than 100 grants to nonprofit organizations. The University of Minnesota Department of Pediatrics was allocated $180,000 in grant money in 2005. In total, the VCF has donated more than four million dollars to support the University of Minnesota Department of Pediatrics, which excels in breakthrough research.

Pat Leopold, coordinator of the Children's Fund, speaks enthusiastically about the Vikings' role in this wonderful charity. As the administrator, he has made valuable contributions to the community, emphasizing the importance of the responsibility to aid community needs.

Brad Madson, director of community relations for the Vikings, truly loves every minute of coordinating such events. His role with the Vikings and community presence is second to none. He is literally a disciple to the community, bringing forth a special gift from his heart to the Vikings every single day.

In the *Vikings Community Report*, Madson states, "The Minnesota Vikings are committed to making our community a better place to live, work, and play through charitable efforts. ... The Minnesota Vikings' popularity allows thousands of opportunities for charities to benefit from the team's success. Donating merchandise and autographed memorabilia to nonprofit groups is another Viking tradition. Examples of the events we support include: school fundraisers, charity auctions, benefits for cancer patients, raffles, and community fundraisers."

The Vikings' desire to reach out is significant to many community organizations. The team receives approximately 300 written requests asking for assistance per week. Occasionally, the Minnesota Vikings' work is even unplanned. Jarren Duffy and his dad had such an experience.

Jarren bought a Vikings jersey bearing the name Koren Robinson and proudly wore it to a game shortly after the purchase. Within a short time after the purchase, Vikings receiver Robinson got into some difficulty and was eventually cut from the team. The jersey suddenly had little value for a proud Viking fan.

Attempts to return the jersey were rebuffed by the store, so Charley Walters, *St. Paul* sports columnist, took on the cause. As a result, many fans across the country wanted to reimburse the Duffys for their loss. This wasn't the family's intention, as they only wanted to return the old jersey for a new one.

All was resolved when Brad Madson heard what happened. On behalf of the Vikings, he called and said he wanted to make it right. Madson invited Jarren and his father, Jeff, to the next Vikings game, gave them seats for the game, and onfield passes.

"It was really something that Brad let us go down onto the field," says Jarren Duffy, recipient of the Vikings' kindness. "I was able to get autographs from former Vikings Bob Lurtsema, Greg Coleman, and Joe Senser."

It was quite a day for the Duffys. And, of course, Jarren watched the game wearing a brand new Chad Greenway jersey, compliments of the Vikings!

The Minnesota Vikings annually give out a Community Quarterback award for volunteerism. In 2002, the award was given to Wayne Kostroski for his magnificent work with Taste of the NFL, which raises money for Second Harvest Heartland Hunger and Solutions of Minnesota.

The Taste of the NFL was founded when Minnesota hosted the 1992 Super Bowl. Since then, Kostroski has been active with the fundraiser in all NFL cities. Kostroski has also been involved with the Vikings in his efforts for many years.

"The Minnesota Vikings are very genuine and different from other cities in that regard. Maybe it's the Minnesota mind-set. There is a character and underlying thread special to what they do," says Kostroski.

Wayne Kostroski has not been involved in his fundraising efforts for the attention or even to directly prove his commitment in helping out the needy. He is involved to draw exposure to the cause and get others to help; he volunteers to become part of the need. If people came forward to give of their time in a small way toward the many needs of the community, there would always be a smile on Wayne Kostroski's face, because he would then know for sure that it has been worthwhile to never give up on his dream. Says Kostroski, "To help someone in need, you don't need a checkbook."

The Minnesota Vikings have found a way to do both. They write checks and donate graciously to many charities and, at the same time, provide countless community hours giving back to those who require it. To provide and assist worthy recipients is a wonderful and deep commitment on their behalf.

The Minnesota Vikings touch the hearts of people in need and organizations in many areas, Smile Network International included. SNI is a Minnesota-based, charitable humanitarian group that provides life-altering reconstructive surgeries to children and young adults in impoverished countries.

The design and major purpose of this wonderful organization is to provide the opportunity to conduct surgical missions abroad and to impart dignity and a quality of life to individuals whose medical needs may otherwise go untreated. The Vikings have been involved extensively in the process.

"The Vikings have been extremely generous with their time and their contributions to Smile Network International. As an organization, they have consistently contributed tickets and memorabilia to Smile Network's live and silent auctions. These donations have helped to raise many thousands of dollars," says Alexis

Walsko of SNI. "It is overwhelming and very powerful to have the Vikings lend their time and support to Smile Network's fundraising efforts. The Vikings bring energy, enthusiasm, and fans to our program. As an organization, Smile Network is always thankful and honored to work in association with them."

The Randy Moss fishing tournament has also been very helpful to the organization in their fundraising efforts. The Vikings invite friends, athletes, and other celebrities to the event. Last year, 50 individuals participated.

The impact of the Vikings franchise on community events is long lasting. Current and past players' contributions are incredible. Many former Viking players are also involved in charity fundraising and proud to continue on the tradition of giving back.

The NFL Alumni Association is a nonprofit service organization of former professional football players who work on a volunteer basis with youth and charity. Many former Vikings are involved with the local chapter, which is directed by former player Kurt Knoff.

The NFL Alumni Association has been "Caring for Kids" for the past 25 years. Along with gaining sponsors and donors and volunteers, making a difference in the lives of at-risk children is a high priority.

"Having the opportunity to provide scholarships to these youths so they can experience YMCA's Camp Menogyn reminds me how we can have an impact on the lives of young people and how much we take for granted. I am grateful to be a part of an organization whose primary goal is 'Caring for Kids,'" says Kurt Knoff, former Minnesota Viking and current president of the Minnesota chapter of the NFL Alumni Association.

When speaking about the Vikings and their incredible community connection, it would be remiss not to mention Linda Louie's passion for the Purple. Louie's connection to the Vikings goes back over 10 years. She has organized and participated in many events where the Men of Purple fame and glory have brought special meaning to those less fortunate.

"Even though the ownership has changed through the years, they have kept alive a community connection," Louie says with deep emotion. "The Viking players have tremendous impact in our area. They have big hearts and they go into the hearts of our community."

"I remember when former Viking Cory Withrow and Spencer Johnson visited Father Tim Vakoc in the hospital," says Louie. "Father Tim had been seriously wounded in Iraq and could not respond.

"After meeting with the players, HE DID RESPOND, AND THE EXCHANGE THEY HAD WAS WONDERFUL," she exclaimed with passionate joy. "The two players said a prayer with him before they left and the Vikings went on a winning streak after that." Little doubt remains in the heart of Linda Louie as to what caused it.

Louie is a double amputee who has built her life around "doing good" for others. She is currently studying pastoral ministry. She exemplifies the spirit of what is right and is unafraid to express her appreciation to those who carry on this spirit. "The Minnesota Vikings are a powerful force in our community that unifies us," she says. "They represent a connection of pride and love for the whole Upper Midwest. They go about helping the 'least' in the community—the people who have no power." To Linda Louie, this is what the organization has been about since her connection with the team began over a decade ago.

Following the Vikings' win and loss column has been a reality since the team's first mark against the Bears in 1961. Most fans only pay attention to such statistics, as the stark reality of a franchise's success is hinged on making the playoffs and advancing to the Super Bowl.

The ultimate success for any NFL franchise is to win the Super Bowl. But a bond exists between the Minnesota Vikings and their community. It is a bond so strong that the recipients of the team's commitment have never-ending praise for the organization and its devotion to better the lives of others.

This is not an organization that just delivers its product on the field each fall. It doesn't just leave the stadium at game's end with a win or loss in popular football standings. This football team believes the game is also played off the field and in a way that truly identifies what is important in life.

In the 46 years since their inception, the Purple have won on life's large playing field. They have played with their hearts and souls and have proven themselves winners. So the next time the Vikings experience a memorable win or endure a disappointing loss, it needs to be recognized that the key to life's success is measured year-round. And the Minnesota Vikings are very special in this regard.

The aforementioned examples of the Vikings' connection to the Minnesota community are only a small sampling of the many contributions they make throughout the weeks, months, and years. In life's standings, they are in first place and winners in every category.

# 6

# PURPLE BOND

"MAYBE IT WAS THE PURPLE PEOPLE EATERS, MAYBE it was the toughness of being outside in the cold weather, or MAYBE it was just because we were the Minnesota Vikings! But I know one thing for sure; we wanted to tell people who we were.

"YOU WANT TO SEE WHAT WE GOT? WELL, COME AND TAKE A LOOK AT US, BECAUSE WE GOT BUD GRANT AND MARSHALL AND PAGE AND ELLER AND TINGELHOFF AND BILL BROWN. AND YOU DON'T HAVE ANYTHING CLOSE TO THAT!"

Above are the words of a huge Viking fan, spoken with great intensity and fervor. It's all there, captured in a passionate accounting that comes from deep within the heart and soul of Mark Thielen, bonded to the Purple forever.

Where does this great passion come from, and how does it become a part of one's spirit? How does it become a temperament and an attitude? It begins as an affair with the Men of Purple, different from most who play the unrestrained and violent game of professional football. It forms a link—a very real, deeply loyal, and forever bonding attachment. And it turns into the love of a franchise, organization, and football team that wears purple each Sunday afternoon.

"The Vikings represent an aggressive toughness generating from the beginning of the franchise's history—a reputation bringing about a passion that consumes you," says Thielen. "And when you are a fan, it is forever, through thick or thin. You're not just a fan when they win. You are a fan during the losses and the difficult times. And I wanted to be a part of it and I still am!

"We had Bud Grant here for 17 years. He was our coach that cemented the bond. He didn't have to demonstrate it; he talked and people listened. He is a leader and a winner, and we just wanted to show him off to others."

A special affiliation between the Minnesota Vikings and their fans has existed over the past 46 years, strengthening as the decades pass. The area has truly embraced this football team. There are many reasons for the affinity and connection, which rose in the '60s and remained locked and shackled into the next century.

In order to fully understand the complexity of this collaboration, one must comprehend the attraction of football and its ability to devour the human soul, turning its very spirit into a lifelong fan.

To many, it is just a passion and fixation, evolving into the reality of their life. The Vikings, on the other hand, have become a major contributor to this infatuation and have bestowed it upon the fans in prodigious fashion.

"It is a family ritual for us," says Molly Ballis, a season ticket holder since 1989. It started at home with our parents watching Viking games on television. We have always cheered for them, always for the Purple!

"On Sundays, we all wear purple. The kids have their purple sweatshirts on and we wear purple gloves if it's cold outside. It's part of being a Minnesotan."

Being one of the Vikings faithful does occasionally have some drawbacks for Molly Ballis. It seems her family's daycare provider happens to be an avid Packers enthusiast, which could cause problems for anyone, especially a Vikings fan.

"If I dress the kids in purple Viking sweatshirts on days they are in day care, she will turn the sweatshirts inside out so she doesn't have to look at the Vikings colors all day," says Ballis.

There should be a rule or some type of penalty against such behavior. The Packers and Vikings—always at odds with each other, even at day care!

Having spent 46 years with the Minnesota Vikings organization, Fred Zamberletti has a theory on the phenomenon. He says, "Football is like an addiction—an addiction being the use of a substance or an event that interferes with your ability to feel. Football is like a legal drug. If someone were to come up to you five minutes before kickoff and say your house is burning down, your spouse has run off with the neighbor, someone has stolen your car from the parking lot … you would tell them … 'Tell me when the game is over at four o'clock.'"

Other theories exist on the incredible relationship between the fans and the Purple. As Bud Grant says about the feverous connection, "The Vikings represent a region, not a city; we are the MINNESOTA Vikings!"

Of the 32 teams in the NFL, the "Minnesota" Vikings are unique. Chicago, Green Bay, Detroit, Dallas, New York (City) Giants, Philadelphia, Washington, New Orleans, Atlanta, Tampa Bay, Seattle, San Francisco, St. Louis, New England, New York (City) Jets, Buffalo, Miami, Indianapolis, Jacksonville, Tennessee, Houston, Baltimore, Cincinnati, Pittsburgh, Cleveland, San Diego, Kansas City, Denver, and Oakland all represent cities.

Additionally, Carolina represents the Carolinas, but they are a relatively new team, as are the Arizona Cardinals, who used to be the St. Louis Cardinals via the Chicago Cardinals. So the fact that the "Minnesota" Vikings' name represents the region is significant to its history and broad base of unparalleled support.

The extraordinary bond likely began at the now torn down Metropolitan Stadium in Bloomington, Minnesota. It was at this historically converted ballpark that Norm Van Brocklin led the Purple to the great upset victory over the Chicago Bears in the franchise's first season opener. Dramatic and unforgettable, it marked the beginning of a winning tradition at Minnesota and a loving affair with its fans.

From this monumental and most memorable victory, a connection grew between variables. The cement had been put in place for the bonding process to begin and for the manacle to bake over the next half-century. The existing factors were significant, and perhaps focused attention on what made the win so special in so many ways.

"When you woke up in the morning after a night in a Bloomington hotel room and heard the wind howling outside and felt the cold air coming into the room through the closed windows, you knew it was going to be a bad day," remembers Fred Cox, former Vikings kicker. "Kicking the football under those conditions was going to be like kicking a brick. I might just as well have gone out and kicked ice chunks!" It was Minnesota pro football in the winter. It was cold and it was nasty!

Vikings football fans grew to love the players, coaches, and the franchise over the incomparable, miserable weather conditions they endured together. But the reasons went beyond this similarity.

First, the purple-clad Vikings were led by the legendary Norm Van Brocklin, who represented greatness and toughness. The fans identified with him. His playing style and his personality were symbolic of the Vikings of old and their heritage. And how the name Vikings came to identify the professional football team of the Northland was soon to be a proud recognition of what the Minnesota Vikings epitomized.

The fighting spirit of the Nordic Vikings and their fearless courage were embedded in the Purple and Van Brocklin. A "will to win" and "street fighter" spirit laid claim to his personality, soon to be recognized and glamorized by the faithful set to follow The Dutchman to fame and glory.

Van Brocklin, the deplorable weather, and Met Stadium were all a part of the area's representation of the NFL in Minnesota. And on those Sunday afternoons in the most frigid weather, fierce rivalries began with the Green Bay Packers and Chicago Bears, the "Monsters of the Midway."

And, of course, the NFL's Central Division, commonly referred to as the "Black and Blue Division," eventually emerged, housing the Packers, the Bears, the Vikings, and the Detroit Lions.

The Purple faithful loved it; the team's tough identity came with being a member of the roughest, meanest, rudest, and most uncivil of divisions in all of professional football.

Qualifying as members of the "Black and Blue Division" came easily for the Packers, Bears, Lions, and Vikings, because players like Ray Nitschke, Dick Butkus, Joe Schmidt, and Lonnie Warwick met all the qualifications, paying dues every Sunday afternoon. They were violent, passionate players with their respective teams and a good fit for the division housing their vocation.

They all performed in wretched and dastardly weather conditions with a "play us and you will pay" attitude. Little choice remained but to love and honor that proclamation. And the fans did.

The bonding process between the Men of Purple and their faithful was in motion. The Viking heritage, cold weather at the Met, Van Brocklin, and the "Black and Blue Division"—it must have been scripted to be so perfect. Someone even wrote "Minnesota Vikings 37, Chicago Bears 13" into the dialogue, solidifying the completeness and perfection of the team's origin.

Former general manager Mike Lynn speaks about the astounding and sensational attraction of the Vikings to the region and their broad fan base, saying, "The Vikings represent the state of Minnesota, the Dakotas, Iowa, and parts of Wisconsin. If there was a poll taken in Canada, I believe the Vikings would win out as the most popular team in the United States."

Why? What makes this relationship so special? No one knows for sure. But whatever the reason, the fact is that it all just falls beautifully into place. The Vikings have always belonged. It just took them a few decades to arrive.

Hearty, stubborn, hardnosed fans willing to brave the elements and most extreme weather conditions to watch a football game in the ice, snow, sleet, and rain qualify as special kinds of people—those loyal to the Purple.

The athletes on the field weren't the only ones who demonstrated true spirit consistent with the team's great Viking heritage; the fans were true Vikings as well. They were proud of the organization and believed in it, and this energizing force has engrossed the past, the present, and the future of this beloved franchise.

The bond grew stronger as the teams got better, and the identity blossomed with Bud Grant in charge. Standing on the sidelines with his stoic and historic look, a Vikings cap and headset, he became the face and fixture of the franchise. And the best was left for last—the Vikings began to win. It wasn't long before winning became the norm and losing the aberration.

The major turnaround for the Minnesota Vikings began in 1969, when a talented, hardnosed burly quarterback by the name of Joe Kapp took the Vikings to the Super Bowl. And he did it not just as a recognized leader of the offense, but rather as a bruising, rugged, do-or-die gridiron giant who preferred to spend weeks recuperating from great, self-inflicted bodily harm than lose a football game.

Smashmouth football—run right at them and make them pay for every tackle attempt—was his goal at quarterback. And he made those in his way pay dearly as he led with a fighting spirit that devoured opponents every Sunday afternoon.

To Vikings fans, Joe Kapp fit right in. He had an edge about him, conquering the weather and opponent in a brazen, take-no-prisoners kind of way symbolic of the Nordic Vikings and all they stood for in their glory days.

Make no mistake about it. Joe Kapp was the leader on this football team. He could have run for governor and won, with the condition that governing would be set aside during the fall. It wouldn't have mattered whether the governor's party was Democrat or Republican, because the process would have been completely bipartisan with No. 11 at the capitol. Who would want to disagree with him? He commanded respect and offered himself up each Sunday with the team's best interests at heart.

Kapp was brought to Minnesota out of the Canadian Football League, where Bud Grant and Jim Finks had become familiar with his swashbuckling style and ferocious desire for ultimate victory.

He was a winner. Once the quarterback at California, he took the Golden Bears to the Rose Bowl. In the Canadian Football League, he quarterbacked the British Columbia Lions to the Grey Cup Championship. And in Minnesota, of course, he led the Vikings to their first Super Bowl.

"All people have in their lives are choices to make in a country like the United States, and if you make the choice to be in football, or in math or music, whatever the choice, you must do it the very best you can," says Kapp. "I was the best I could be in a tough, violent game and I learned the lesson from my mother, Florence Garcia Kapp, who taught me if I am going to do something, to do it the very best I can."

When the former quarterback speaks those words he so believes in, he does it with the same passion that, when in pursuit of the goal line, drove his head and body into anyone in his way. Changes to the body slow a person down as the years pass, but the fierce passion within Joe Kapp doesn't understand the aging process.

If all it took for pro football success today was desire, loyal fans of the bruising Purple quarterback would be unable to rule out the possibility that he might play again someday, some four decades later.

One thing is for sure. Telling the athlete that he didn't make the team wouldn't be a pleasant experience. Cutting Joe Kapp from the roster might be best accomplished by just slipping a note under his door, rather than speaking to him in person. The passion he shows for his beliefs remains second to none.

After the 1969 season, Kapp coined the phrase "40 for 60"—40 players on the Vikings' roster pulling together for 60 minutes of a game. In his eyes, there were no stars. They were all great players and leaders, and none would be successful without the others. He practiced it, he believed in it, and it became a part of Vikings football, adding to the cement bonding everything else together in proud tradition.

The passion behind this phrase came from Kapp's experience in college as the 12th man on California's basketball team. "Pete Newell and Rene Herrerias, the Cal coaches, made me feel as important on the team as any other player. And I was," said Kapp.

Joe Kapp's famous "40 for 60 " motto has traveled four decades with the franchise. Long before he made the statement, it was an integral part of his inner being, and continues to remain so.

Kapp speaks with great love for his former Viking teammates. "When I came to the Vikings, you couldn't find better players than those like Mick Tingelhoff, Jim Marshall, Carl Eller, Bill Brown, and Dave Osborn. But it was all of us pulling together as a team to win the game, '40 for 60,' which is why we were successful," says Kapp. "There was no one ever happier than me in my work. You take the relationships that we earned, and all 40 of us could look each other in the eyes and know who we were."

Minnesota was significant to Kapp and he loved the fans. "The Minnesota Vikings fans are very strong, almost like a cult. Everywhere I go in the country, there are Vikings fans. Returning to Minnesota is always very special to me. The fans were a part of our success," says Kapp, "it was the team and the community."

The former athlete now lives in California. His great passion for football remains, as he frequently is involved in public speaking and fundraising as a consultant to projects related to education. An integral part of Viking football and the bond it has created, Joe Kapp was a major force in connecting with the fans and will continue to live on in great Vikings lore.

Snapping the ball from the center position for Joe Kapp was Mick Tingelhoff, who played for the Vikings for 17 years. Tingelhoff loved playing in Minnesota and has made his home in the state since retirement.

"Minnesota people always treated us well," say Tingelhoff. "They are great fans who continue to recognize the older players. I have never experienced a negative moment from a fan in all the years I have played and lived here. This is a great place to live and to have played."

It is something very special to Mick Tingelhoff to have played for the Minnesota Vikings. He takes great pride in it. "Once you are a Viking, you will always be a Viking," he says with such delight and gratification.

Tingelhoff retired in 1978, and still receives three to four fan letters a week. "It means a lot to me when someone comes up to me and recognizes me as a Viking, and it is an honor for someone to ask me for an autograph," he says.

If a solid focal point was instrumental in bonding the Vikings and their supporters, it likely began with Mick Tingelhoff. Soft spoken with a good heart, he is a wonderful person. The honor he felt playing for the Vikings and his reputation with the fans was important to him. "Because the Minnesota people recognize you as a Viking, it is important to be a good person," he believes.

Setting an example and never doing anything to tarnish the team's image is a high priority for the great Vikings center. And he is magnificently symbolic of what the Purple franchise has stood for since its entry into the NFL.

He started 240 consecutive games and never missed a start in the 17 years he played in Minnesota. One of the legendary quotes about the durable Vikings center came from his back up, Godfrey Zaunbrecher, during the 1971 to 1973 seasons when he stated, "I am the third-string center on a team that has only two centers on the roster. I play behind Tingelhoff and Tingelhoff hurt." The comment contained humor; unfortunately for Zaunbrecher, however, the statement was also true. Mick Tingelhoff's durability was unquestioned.

The relationship the players had with the fans in the Vikings' early years has carried through for many decades and is significant to the bonding love affair that exists today.

Many of these players have taken great pride and satisfaction in doing their job both on and off the field. Stu Voigt is one of them. Voigt, a recognizable name in the Twin Cities for his active role in charity events and media work covering the Vikings, has always been synonymous with all that is right about the Purple.

Voigt has a fierce loyalty to the team and organization. He deeply wanted to be a member of the Vikings and carried the honor with credible passion during his 11 years, wearing purple from 1970 to 1980. He was a magnificent player and has been a charismatic credit to the organization since retirement.

Voigt believes the Vikings' tradition has been incredibly strong through the decades. He joined the Vikings out of the University of Wisconsin at the age of 21 and received valuable, unforgettable lessons about life from the team's veterans.

Voigt speaks of the "Viking way," a decision-making process that made the team special. "Bud looked for good guys who could make plays," he says. "And he found them in the Tingelhoffs, the Ellers, and Gary Larson."

Voigt appreciated his fellow players and the coaches, and recognized the mission to encourage players to reach out to the community and the fans. "The fans were always there for us, and we owed it to them to give something back," says Voigt.

It is very rare for Stu Voigt to miss an alumni charity event. He is always there, carrying on the pride and character of the Vikings for both the past and present. The instilling, inspirational focus Voigt has regarding "respect for the game" is compelling and insightful. He truly understands the importance of being a good person and demonstrates this in everything he does. He grasps the magnitude of players' roles within the community and the image they should portray.

Voigt has high regard for the Minnesota faithful. "They are very loyal, hearty Midwestern types in a Vikings town, no question about it," Voigt says in a proud and gracious manner.

"I owe a great deal of gratitude to the Minnesota Vikings," he continues. "There is something to putting on the Viking uniform, a real legacy! I have the same pride in the Vikings today as when I played." This has never been in doubt. All one has to do is spend some time with Stu Voigt to see the passion, enthusiasm, and appreciation he has for his ability to have played the game in a purple uniform.

Voigt was also a good friend of another area icon that found his way into the hearts of the Purple fans. He was Voigt's roommate when they traveled and they had a great relationship. His name was Fran Tarkenton.

Extraordinary and most memorable, Tarkenton held the reins for the Purple from 1961 to 1976 and again from 1972 to 1978. He made the game interesting and enjoyable from beginning to end. Although he had an ability to turn conservative game planning and play calling to instant glory or ruin, he made things happen and was a sensational crowd pleaser.

Voigt recalls rooming with "the Scrambler" as being quite an experience. During one of their trips out of town with the team, Reggie Jackson and Howard Cosell paid Tarkenton a visit. Just as Voigt was getting over the fascination of the celebrity visits to their room, the telephone rang. President Gerald Ford was on the line, and he wasn't asking to talk to Voigt. It was never a dull day around Francis Tarkenton.

Former Vikings coach Jerry Burns has great regard for his ex-signal caller. Burns was the offensive coordinator when No. 10 became the field leader. "Francis and I always had a great relationship," says Burns. "I gave him everything he wanted!"

Fans' love for the Minnesota Vikings and their prowess on the field is historic. But it doesn't just go one way. As proven by Voigt and Tingelhoff, appreciation for fans comes from the players as well. Both are unified with a common goal, and the mutual affection they show one another has made the relationship special.

"The Twin Cities is a great place," remarks Jerry Burns, one of the most colorful and loved coaches in Vikings history. "It is very meaningful to me. It is special here. There are great people and great recreational opportunities. You can't beat this area to live in. My family lives here and loves it, and I have eight of my 15 grandchildren living close by. This is our home."

If you ask someone to tell you about Jerry Burns, three things will occur in almost every instance. First, the recipient of the request for information will smile. Next, some affectionate form of laughter will be heard. And finally, the comment, "What a great guy," will follow. The former coach has a trademark of credibility and colleagues and friends are deeply fond of him.

Burns has memorable and positive reflections on the connection between the Vikings and their fans. In his eyes, it is something unique. "There is a great relationship between the people here and the Minnesota Vikings," he says. And when Jerry Burns shows such a deep appreciation for the area and the fans, it comes from personal experience, gratitude, and high regard.

The Vikings have held training camp at Mankato State University for the past 42 years. Second longest in the NFL, this period of longevity makes the Vikings and the city proud partners. Mankato, located about a two-hour drive south of the Twin Cities, has been the second home for the Purple before each season and is filled with memories.

Fans remember the autograph sessions and the ability to watch practices in close proximity. But sometimes a totally unscheduled event would take place during a practice. The Vikings' "old benchwarmer," Bob Lurtsema, remembers how he made one long day interesting.

The defensive linemen were lined up, ready to hit the blocking sled. As each player took his turn and charged into the sled, the impact could be heard throughout Mankato. The sled contained several padded posts in a row and each hit on the pad required a subsequent turn in a circle, a driving hit on the next pad, until the end of the sled and the last blocking pad faced the collision.

Lurtsema drove into the first pad, turned and hit the next pad, turned and hit the next pad, and continued to do so until he reached the end. Instead of returning to the beginning of the line to start over after the last turn, he added a little something special to the drill. He faced the fence, which sectioned off the practice area from spectators and a group of youngsters who were enjoying the practice session.

Lurtsema looked directly at the kids, put a thumb in each ear, and wildly waved his hands, sticking his tongue out at them. No one could believe it! Right in front of their very eyes was a member of the Minnesota Vikings football team mocking them during practice.

Vikings football practice … a huge defensive lineman in uniform … and this! The fans were shocked and surprised.

When Lurtsema reached the end of the line and turned toward the fence the next time through the drill, the same group of kids all stood with thumbs in their ears, waving their hands and sticking out their tongues at the "old benchwarmer."

Instead of returning to the line for a subsequent attack on the blocking sled, this time Lurtsema ran toward the kids, jumped the fence, and chased the disrespectful lot into the parking area.

Although the coaches yelled at Lurtsema for his modification during the practice period, it was well worth the fun he had with the kids. Lurtsema loves to tell the story. If one of those youngsters could be found, they would probably share it too, even some 30 years later!

Bob Lurtsema is a warm-hearted, energetic symbol of Viking football, and beloved for his characterization as the "old benchwarmer." Although he has made a career out of crediting himself for never playing, his victimization is much overplayed, because he was an outstanding football player. However, rarely ever on the "front lines" to do battle on Sundays, he did give fans plenty of ammunition to sympathize with his role on the bench.

Lurtsema even found that his self-described analysis as a benchwarmer occasionally caused opposing players to overlook him. The Vikings were playing the Detroit Lions when Lurtsema was sent into the game early in the first quarter—a very unusual occurrence. After all, if you sat behind the famed Purple People Eaters, Alan Page, Jim Marshall, Carl Eller, Gary Larson, and later Doug Sutherland, you wouldn't expect to play very much either, especially in the first quarter.

But on this day, Lurtsema was sent into the game. On his first play, he crashed through the line in ferocious style, sacking Lions quarterback Bill Munson on the turf. Delivering a fierce hit, Lurtsema had done his job to perfection.

It was a terrific play—one for the highlight films and a lifelong memory. Lurtsema knew what a great play he had made. His mind raced with thoughts of highlight reels on Sports Center, ESPN, and the local channels. It was exactly what he was paid to do, and he did it during primetime in an unforgettable fashion. The drama and excitement, however, were not long lasting.

As Lurtsema lay on the ground enjoying the moment, the Detroit quarterback looked up at him and said, "My ... are we that far behind already that you're in the game?"

Lurtsema has always been very popular among the Purple faithful. He loves the game and all that goes with it, and has always felt that to be able to share his experience with the fans is of the greatest importance. He also believes it is a true honor to be asked for an autograph.

He recalls the time a man in his mid-60s asked if he could shake his hand. The request, which came many years after he had retired, demonstrates the respect the former athlete still holds and "meant more to me than to the fan," says Lurtsema.

Maybe Lurtsema's perspective on this action comes from an all-star event he attended while in high school. Speaking at the function was Baltimore Orioles pitcher Milt Pappas. At the end of the evening, Pappas touched Lurtsema's hand on his way out.

"Milt Pappas spoke at the event and walked by me on the way out. I held my hand out and he slicked my hand with his. Did he look at me? No. Does he remember today touching my hand? No way! But I remember, and I still remember what it meant to me. What I do is remembered by people," said Lurtsema.

One of the ex-player's fondest memories comes from a fan who was very ill. After receiving a letter from Lurtsema, she remarked that she had enjoyed the best three days of her life in over a year. Going

---

The old benchwarmer, Bob Lurtsema, and his antics helped strengthen the bond that exists between the Vikings and their fans.
*Photo courtesy of the Minnesota Vikings*

out of one's way for others pays dividends and rewards far beyond any expectation.

A very special connection exists in the state of Minnesota between the Vikings football team and the city of Mankato. Other rare moments have occurred there, stuffed in the far end of the memory bank only to be heard by a select few. One such story is legendary and initially created quite a stir.

"LOOK OVER THERE, UP ON THE ROOF OF THE BUILDING! IT'S MILLARD AND KIFFIN FIGHTING!" This frightening cry rang out from the Vikings' practice field as assistant coach Monte Kiffin and defensive tackle Keith Millard were observed brawling on the top of a several-story building.

As an assistant under both Jerry Burns and Dennis Green, Monte Kiffin was with the Vikings from 1986 to 1989 and 1991 to 1994. He was an extremely knowledgeable and disciplined coach who put together some great defensive plans for the Vikings, and Keith Millard was one of his best players. But the two of them were notorious for getting into each other's faces during the heat of battle, most often at practice.

A great player out of Washington State, Millard came to the Vikings after a short stint with Jacksonville in the World Football League. For a defensive lineman, he had the perfect attitude— ferocious, with a motor stuck in high gear inside of him. Big and well conditioned, he was a fan's treasure on Sunday afternoons and an offensive lineman's nightmare when assigned to block him. He knew what was expected of him and played a nasty brand of violent football.

During one practice session at training camp, Millard and Kiffin got after each other, and the argument rose to flaming proportions. Jerry Burns stepped into the middle of it and screamed in wrath at Millard, "Get off the field, and if this ever happens again, you are out of here!" Those within hearing range had no doubt that the head coach had had enough of Millard's behavior.

Millard left the area in a rage, and as the practice came to an end, Kiffin soon followed. Several players were kept on the field to work on "special team drills." About 20 minutes after Millard and Kiffin left the practice area, one of the players shouted out that the two were fighting on the roof.

It was unbelievable! As players and coaches watched on the field, Keith Millard and Monte Kiffin, an assistant coach, were brawling on top of a tall building adjacent to the practice field. And then it happened. As described by one of the observers, "OH MY … MILLARD THREW KIFFIN OFF THE ROOF!" They watched as Kiffin fell several stories, crashing to the ground.

The rest of the day went according to schedule with little disruption. Millard went about his business, as did the rest of the team, although the incident was discussed. In fact, many years later, the story still comes up from time to time.

Fortunately, no one had to call the police or a medical examiner. No one had to find the remains of the victim. No one had to impose any discipline on the Vikings' big defensive giant. You see, the tumbling body from the roof wasn't really Monte Kiffin, it was only a dummy made up to look like the lineman's coach.

Many who watched the scene or heard about it afterwards never knew for sure who actually made the dummy that looked like Monte Kiffin. They never knew who cooked up the practical joke, Kiffin or Millard. Or was it Jerry Burns' idea?

The answer to the puzzle comes from longtime Vikings equipment manager, Dennis Ryan. "Jerry Burns had me go to Sears and buy a mannequin. I hauled that thing to Mankato and back for three years, waiting for Burns to say it was the right moment for the elaborate hoax. It was dressed and made up to look like Monte Kiffin," says Ryan. "Jerry Burns is the funniest man I have ever met."

Such practical jokes prove that a bond not only exists between players and fans, but also within the organization itself. Former Vikings punter and current radio analyst Greg Coleman understands this connection well. Of his time with the Vikings, Coleman says, "It was such a special time in my life because I knew I had one of only 32 jobs in the world, and being the first African American to hold the position was special."

Coleman has great memories of the organization and those people who made an impact on him. "Bud Grant could be a complicated person if you couldn't look past his stone-faced demeanor," explains Coleman. "He was a stickler for detail. He would observe the little things about the game of football that many people would overlook, but it was those little things that led to much of his success as a Hall of Fame coach."

Coleman also has a great deal of respect for Jerry Burns. "He was a coach that was concerned about one thing: winning. He had one of the greatest football minds I've seen," Coleman says.

Coleman speaks of his wonderful association with other longtime Vikings, like equipment manager Dennis Ryan and trainer Fred Zamberletti. "Fred taught me how to take care of my body and was a great sounding board who was full of wisdom and common sense. And Dennis Ryan, he did whatever it took to make sure players had what they needed, even if they didn't know it."

Coleman represents the organization well, hosting a fundraising golf tournament each year, among other things. "You feel as a player a responsibility to give back something because the community has stuck with you through thick and thin," he says.

A major part of the Vikings' foundation is based on the belief that their responsibilities include such commitments to their supporters. "Bud created the loyalty to each other and to the fans," says Bob Lurtsema. "He brought together the respect we have for each other. We did things for the fans—and still do today—because it is the right thing to do. We realize the love in our soul and feel how lucky we are."

Former Vikings kicker Fred Cox speaks of being a role model. He clearly understands his part as a former Viking and how much it has meant to fans through the years. "I have been retired for 30 years, and get about 700 fan letters a year," he says. "Who would have thought I would get one?"

Cox says fans write many letters regarding great Vikings memories. "When the fans came out and cheered us on, they were in the game," says Cox. "We owed something to the fans. We were just regular guys and we got it across to the fans that way. We just played football.

"The fans found an attachment to us and they felt they could relate to us, and we were going to give it everything we had to win for them!" says Cox. "No heaters, no gloves, no nothing. In the eyes of the fans, we were real Vikings!"

The Minnesota Vikings have meant a great deal to many people who have grown up watching the Purple perform in the fall season. One of these individuals is Mike Max, longtime Twin Cities' sports reporter. "I remember going to the games with my dad at the old Met," says Max. Like many others who have followed the Vikings, his memories never seem to fade.

As a young boy, Max's favorite player was Fran Tarkenton; however, Bud Grant may now be the most exceptional to him. "Of all the people I have covered in my sports career, I learned the most from Bud," says Max. "He made life so simple. 'Don't complicate it.' He was the ultimate leader."

Max recalls a time when Grant had the players pick up rocks off the field—not because it was a necessary task, but because he wanted to break up the routine. Once, the head coach also allowed his team to play basketball at Mankato when it was raining.

One former player Mike Max deeply admires is Stu Voigt. "He is so intelligent and he was never overwhelmed by the game. He has been one of the great ambassadors for the team," says Max.

From his days as a young boy visiting the home of the Vikings to his team coverage today, Mike Max remains passionate when speaking of the Viking history and tradition.

Names from the past like Jim Marshall, Carl Eller, Tingelhoff, Bill Brown, Tarkenton, Cox, Alan Page, Ron Yary, and Paul Krause, recent and present players including Cris Carter, Daunte Culpepper, Randy Moss, and Matt Birk, and others have helped to cement together a bond that has grown since the Vikings first took the field in 1961.

But others have participated in capturing the magic that has ensued from the magnificent Purple over the decades, especially Hub Meeds, the original Vikings mascot. Many great Purple fans have certainly existed throughout the Vikings' reign in the Northland. But no others can boast that they have been featured on the Viking Media Guide or the Vikings' schedules, nor can they claim the title of "THE VIKING"—except Hub Meeds, of course.

January 11, 1970, holds significant distinction in Minnesota Vikings history and lore. True, it is the day the great 1969 team fell to the Kansas City Chiefs at the Superdome in New Orleans, Louisiana, in the Purple's first Super Bowl appearance. But it is also the day Hub Meeds was cast as the first Vikings mascot, both prematurely and without permission.

Meeds and his brother-in-law, Dan Jeans, traveled to the big game in rented Vikings costumes. The look they portrayed was so original and magnetic that upon arrival, they were ushered through a pass gate and onto the field by unsuspecting personnel, who figured they must have been authorized and connected to the Vikings.

The mascot's origin marked the beginning of a fame that would last for the better part of 20 years. A letter to the Vikings the following spring was followed up by permission to attend the games and exhibit the Vikings' passion from the sidelines.

The Vikings contributed to this passion with tickets, sideline passes, and a trip to one away game. And Meeds performed well. He knew how to get the crowd in a frenzy and had a great sense of timing in the process. Meeds would lift his sword and shield, bellowing out an incredulous roar, and the faithful would provide the rest of the noise. Raising his arms and leaning back with a sword raised upwards toward the sky, Meeds supplied the impetus for the crowd to "roar on the Vikings."

The shield, horns, burlap undergarment, fake fur boots with leather strips, and imitation sheepskin vest were all part of the carefully designed, handmade garb that made Meeds' famous costume Viking-like.

Meeds' wife, Patty, and a neighbor, carefully crafted an outfit that put the man into Viking tradition and honor for many years to come. But it wasn't just the look and field placement that made

Long since retiring, Hub Meeds puts on "The Viking" gear once more.

Meeds special. It was his uncanny knack for getting a rise out of the crowd at the precise moment its noise could make a difference.

The record books don't reflect it, but history knows that Hub Meeds was likely responsible for many of the great Vikings victories. Meeds was a leader of the "12th Man" fame and performed his responsibility in the highest tradition.

The look and passion he exhibited during Vikings games made Hub Meeds as regular a fixture along the sidelines as Gatorade, benches, the Men in Purple, and even Bud Grant. He was a bookend and major part of the past, keeping the bond between the Vikings and their fans tightly closed.

Meeds is retired now, but still has the Vikings' great passion for winning each Sunday. He is a wonderful family man. Soft spoken, he does not appear to be the type who would rally a crowd and a team, as he did so magnificently behind his mighty Vikings wear throughout so many seasons.

His Sunday mornings no longer involve dressing up to cheer on the Vikings. Free from the horns, the giant Vikings shield, and the cold of the old Metropolitan Stadium in Bloomington, he ushers the eight o'clock Mass near his home in White Bear Lake, Minnesota.

As he walks down the aisle so graciously assisting parishioners to their seats and taking up the collection, though, one has to wonder if, for just an instant, he would like to rear back, throw up his arms, cast his mighty sword and shield high into the air, and bellow out a bone-crushing cheer for the Vikings once again. It might upset the Mass, but it would be worth it.

Other Viking loyalists also take their passion a step further than most when it comes to expressing their devotion. For one member of the faithful, Sunday home games begin a ritual at approximately 9:45 in the morning.

"First, I take a shower and then I begin by putting on my Vikings boxer shorts," says Kim Lokken, avid Vikings follower. "Next comes another pair of Vikings regular shorts, followed by Vikings socks and Vikings pants. Over my Vikings T-shirt is my Vikings jersey. Next comes the Vikings hat with Vikings metals and jewelry." On a side note, if the Vikings win on Sunday, boxer shorts washed on a regular basis will be worn again and again until a loss.

Next, Lokken and his wife, Betty, are ready to head off to the game. But first, magnetic insignias need to be put on the car and flags need to be attached to the windows.

Lokken has a Vikings collection beyond the imagination. His entire basement, bathroom, closets, and two bedrooms are filled with belongings that convey his passionate love for the Vikings. There aren't enough pages here to record it all, but the space includes footballs, helmets, purple chairs, shirts, jackets, hats, pictures, plaques, trophies, lamps, rugs, pillows, blankets, bedspreads, a Vikings train set, a grill, toys, posters, signs, ornaments, programs, and ticket stubs from every game attended.

Lokken tapes every Vikings game and watches each one. He has St. Paul and Minneapolis newspapers detailing every game the Vikings have played. If you were to wander into his basement bathroom, you would step on a Viking rug and see many toilet articles, such as a purple toilet seat, Vikings toothpaste and brush, cologne, spray, and a Vikings tissue box, among other things.

If you are lucky, Lokken might set up his homemade Vikings train track and run his Vikings train, which sits on a purple covered pool table. Lying on a small table is a Vikings candy dish with purple and gold candy inside. His dog eats from a Vikings dog dish.

Following the Vikings his whole life has enhanced his fervor. "It is stronger than ever," Lokken says. "I went to my first Viking game when I was 12 and have held the passion for 40 years!" Even during a brief period when he moved with his family to Michigan, the Vikings remained in his heart. He has missed only one game since 1985.

Lokken never leaves a game early, and is disgusted with fans who come to the games wearing no Viking apparel or the jersey of a player who has been traded. Lokken's dream in life is for the Vikings to someday win the coveted Super Bowl. "Everything I ever loved about sports will have come full circle if that happens," he says. "My team will finally have won."

And if he happens to have died before that occurs? "Then my family and all my friends will know that I am smiling down from above," explains Lokken. When the Vikings win, he is as happy as can be. And when they lose, "I get a lump in my throat which makes it hard for me to swallow." A true, diehard Vikings fan, Kim Lokken might just demonstrate the bond that exists between the faithful and the Purple better than anyone else.

When taking a close look at the past 46 years of Vikings football, it is easy to recognize the importance of the Purple. But identifying the special bond cemented from one NFL season to the next and why the community has embraced the Minnesota franchise in such a powerful manner launches quite a discussion.

Having been trained well by the great Minnesota Gophers teams of the early '60s, the Northland had a pretty fair understanding of football. The area had become accustomed to winning, as legendary coach Murray Warmath took the maroon and gold to two consecutive Rose Bowls. With the likes of Carl Eller, Bobby Bell, and Sandy Stephens, football was a familiar event on Saturday afternoons.

On Sundays, the Packers were around—at least, closer than anyone else—and a little about the pro game was learned from them. Minnesota knew about the famed quarterback Norm Van Brocklin. When he took the reins of the Purple in a monumental win over the Bears, it was a grand beginning.

Old Met Stadium endured harsh weather conditions, but Harry Peter "Bud" Grant and the players he governed soon became household names. A touch of victory on Sunday afternoons eventually brought divisional championships, big playoff wins, and four Super Bowls, forging the mammoth depth of interest and passion. And the players played and they stayed, some together for 10 years or more, and many remained in the area after retirement.

Then there were the games that really seemed to cement the bond. All contributed to the Vikings' renowned history—the dreadful Dallas loss as well as the great Kramer-to-Rashad pass to beat the Browns and send the Vikings to the playoffs.

Few will ever forget that great call from legendary announcer Ray Scott as Kramer prepared to throw the bomb down the field in the historic Cleveland game. ... "Five seconds left ... Kramer back to pass ... he's throwing deep ... down the right sideline ... for Rashad ... TOUCHDOWN! TOUCHDOWN! RASHAD!" Vikings fans will never forget the call or the finish—one of the GREATEST EVER!

Maybe it all came together simply because it was meant to be. But whatever the reason, 46 years later there is no doubt that the passion and love remain ... in PURPLE BOND.

# 7

# PURPLE
# PASSION

ABOUT 40 YEARS AGO, it is possible that the following scenario could have occurred. A friend calls and invites you to the Minnesota Vikings game on Sunday—your first professional football game. You have heard about the Men in Purple, read about them, watched them on television, and listened to their games on the radio. But this will be your first game in person.

In anticipation of your first Vikings football game, you might wonder about the cost of the tickets, the seat location, or what kind of clothing to wear. Among other questions associated with watching your gridiron heroes in person, you might ask yourself, "Do we have 50-yard line seats? How far is the stadium entrance from where we will park the car? How much does the food cost?"

A day or so before the game, your friend tells you to wear old, lightweight clothing, even though the weather is likely to be cold, and to bring a pair of gloves with a good grip. Sounds odd, but you give it little concern, because you are going to your first Vikings game! What does it matter what you wear or bring with you? Everything will be wonderful!

It does become a little disconcerting, however, when your friend mentions to you that there are no tickets for the game. Your entry into the stadium will be slightly unorthodox and highly controversial. You and your friend will enter Metropolitan Stadium in Bloomington, Minnesota, by climbing a light pole over the fence.

The plan will be to continue to move around during the game to avoid ushers who may want to assist you with your seat location or ask you for your tickets.

This is a troubling situation at best, but experience dictates it to be a good method for attending a Vikings game. And it probably never really happened quite as described, although it may have had you gone to the game with Dennis Berry of Maplewood, Minnesota.

You see, Berry, one of the greatest Vikings fans ever, has actually climbed a light pole for entrance into Metropolitan Stadium, where his beloved Minnesota Vikings were preparing to play.

"Back when I was in high school in the late '60s, we didn't have a lot of money, but my friends and I loved the Vikings," says Berry. "It was expensive for us to get tickets for the game, so we would go out to the old Met Stadium and wait until the game started, then climb the light poles to get in. We would have to keep moving once we got into the stadium, because there never were any empty seats, so we had to stay ahead of security. Finally, they caught on and started greasing the poles so we couldn't climb them anymore."

*Webster's New Universal Unabridged Dictionary* defines passion, in part, as "any powerful or compelling emotion or feeling as love or hate." Dennis Berry's passion for the Purple is exemplary, and he literally ran with it many decades ago.

Berry is a gigantic Vikings fan whose loyalty spans over four decades. Although the Vikings lost to Kansas City in the 1970 Super Bowl, they were triumphant over the Chiefs the following year at home in Bloomington. Berry was at the game.

"The Vikings won that game by a huge amount, and it made us think that our Vikings were the best team if they could beat the champions from the year before. This was the early years of the Bud Grant dynasty, so we were just starting to understand how good this team was," says Berry, whose devotion to the team was just beginning.

Berry went to a few more games as time passed, but watched most of them on television. Some years after the Vikings' first Super Bowl defeat, he took his wife to her first game, which was a playoff against Dallas following the 1975 season. This matchup was infamous—one of the most historic and unforgettable in Viking history.

"This is the game that Drew Pearson caught the 'Hail Mary' pass that ruined our season," remarks Berry. "It was a horrible day. We were in the old, black bleacher cheap seats. These were the coldest seats in the house. I remember thinking how we had the game won when we had the Cowboys with a fourth and long with a minute left. The play that got the first down for the Cowboys was almost as big a play as the 'Hail Mary.' Things turned ugly. ... Then, from out of the stands comes a beer bottle and hits the official in the head, and my wife and I were scared. This isn't supposed to happen."

Not only was it one of the most devastating losses in Vikings history, but also a dreadful experience for any in the stadium that fateful afternoon. The crowd's reaction to the shenanigans on the field and the aftermath of the disaster is a painful recollection.

Vikings fans attending the game will live with the aftermath, and those who faithfully listened on the radio or watched the game on television will also have the results permanently etched in their memories.

But there would be more pleasant experiences for Berry as his passion and loyalty to the Men of Purple continued. He lived near Midway Stadium in St. Paul, where the Vikings once practiced, and used to watch them on the way home from work. It was always a pleasant experience and, at times, he even had the opportunity to interact with the players.

His love affair continues with the Vikings and the connection is as strong as ever. Traveling to road games, playoff games, and the Pro Bowl in Hawaii are all part of the Purple lifestyle. Berry wears Vikings colors most days, has tons of memorabilia, and is making a Vikings room in his cabin. Berry is a good fit with the Minnesota Vikings, but he is not alone. Another Vikings loyalist from Indiana joins in Berry's fervor.

So you think you have great passion for the Vikings? Did you tell your parents that you wanted to be buried at midfield at the old Metropolitan Stadium? Every time you see or hear a number, do you think of a Viking who has worn it? Do you have numbers on your cell phone signifying a Vikings' pass completion? Do you put purple lights on your Christmas tree?

Scott Angel from Crown Point, Indiana, may be the origin of such questions, but he still has all of the correct answers.

Angel once told his parents that, if he died first, he would like to be buried at midfield at Metropolitan Stadium in Bloomington, Minnesota, the former home of the Minnesota Vikings football team. A few years back, he visited the Mall of America where the old stadium site stood, perhaps looking for the location he had once planned as his burial plot. Could there be any better place to rest in peace than beneath a field where the Purple People Eaters once roamed?

No. 83 ... Stu Voigt ... No. 81 ... Carl Eller. It's an easy game for Scott Angel. And, when Angel got his cell phone a couple years ago, the faithful were pretty used to Daunte Culpepper's passes to Randy Moss. It only made common sense for the last four numbers of Angel's cell phone to be 1184, or "Culpepper to Moss!"

Along with the lights on his Christmas tree, Scott Angel is solid purple—make no mistake about it. His devotion began as he watched the great Fran Tarkenton scramble around on Sundays. Angel was very fast as a youngster, so he quickly identified with No. 10. In fact, he wore No. 10 in basketball, baseball, and football all four years in high school in honor of the great Vikings Hall of Fame inductee.

In honor of his infatuation for the Purple, Angel's home includes a Vikings bathroom complete with a Vikings shower curtain and soap dispenser. His family's holiday plans center around the team's schedule, and winning always makes the Christmas season better.

When Angel played in a competitive touch football league a few years back, his teammates felt the need to remove his shoelaces from his shoes after a Vikings loss, fearing that Angel might potentially have suicidal tendencies after the defeat.

Vikings football was even a priority over Scott Angel's place of employment. He used to sell used cars and recalls watching the Vikings on television in his office while customers on the lot looked for someone to help them. One could surmise the customers weren't deserving of assistance if they didn't possess enough decency and respect for the Purple to stay home and watch the game.

Angel once accepted the fact that his behavior was uncalled for in response to a Viking loss and paid for the damages his frustration caused. In this case, however, the fan's behavior could have been regarded as acceptable under the circumstances.

When Nathan Poole caught an infamous touchdown pass in the corner of the end zone on the last play of a playoff game in 2004, knocking the Vikings out of the race, Angel pushed over a table and broke a few items. For Scott Angel and countless others, though, such spirited actions are all in the best interest of the Purple!

If there were a Hall of Fame for ushers, Dick Jonckowski would be a charter member. While on the sidelines at the old Metropolitan Stadium from 1962 to 1978, Jonckowski caught 112 field goals and eight errant passes. He was famous for his "behind the back pass" as he returned each ball to the officials. Jim Finks, former Vikings general manager, once even told him to "keep it up!" The crowds loved his flare and often responded with loud cheers as Jonckowski performed.

Jonckowski works for the University of Minnesota, serving as the "Voice of the Gophers" for basketball and baseball, and is one of the all-time great emcee speakers at various events and fundraisers. Jonckowski's passion for the Vikings began with the team's entry into Minnesota lore. His knowledge of the players, coaches, and great games of the past is legendary.

As an usher, Jonckowski's recall of stadium incidents is incredible. His memory proves that someone was always trying to sneak into a Vikings game. Take the man dressed as a priest who came in to say a prayer, only to be found out for his trickery—the real priest had entered the same gate minutes before.

In all of Vikings history, maybe the best attempt to enter a game was made by a man who arrived at the gate with a bucket of ice. He hurriedly told Jonckowski, "I'm working for the Detroit Lions and I need to bring the bucket of ice to the Lions' dressing room." The usher replied, "We are playing the Bears!"

Local residents are not the only ones with a passion for the Minnesota Vikings. One of the largest fan clubs is located in Southern California and run by Phil Pusateri. With the help of former Hall of Fame tackle Ron Yary, Pusateri has been a key ingredient in keeping Purple supporters active on the West Coast for many years.

Pusateri speaks with great passion and love for the organization when referencing the team's support for their club. "They bend over backwards to help us," says Pusateri, "and they are really people's people."

The club's current membership includes over 280 individuals, and they regularly attend Vikings training camp and a game in the Twin Cities every year. Loyalty is the nucleus of this organization, which bleeds the purple many miles west of Minnesota.

But you don't have to be in any fan club to love the Vikings. Lori Markuson is proof of that. She has only missed one Vikings game in 27 years. She sits in the stands every Sunday, cheering on the Purple in a Scott Studwell jersey—the second one she has owned, as the first wore out.

"The Vikings are the heart and soul of the community," says Markuson. "It is not about a person, but a team, and we have to support them, win or lose." However, some players might be just a little more special to Markuson than others.

"It is about loyalty to a team, like Scott Studwell had to the Vikings. He played here his whole career and gave everything he had. He always had blood on his pants," says Markuson proudly. "He truly embodied the spirit of the game." Lori Markuson's statement represents a great tribute to a great player from a great fan.

Michaelle Battig calls herself the "greatest Viking fan," and she would certainly be a frontrunner. She even has proof to back up her claim.

"My son Travis decided to enter this Vikings world two weeks early. The doctors wanted to induce labor at noon, but the Vikings

A major part of the organization over the years, former Viking Scott Studwell is still highly respected by the fans. *Photo courtesy of the Minnesota Vikings*

had a noon kickoff and I made them wait until the game was over before inducing labor," explains Battig. "I was able to catapult my son's birth into worldwide 'Minnesota Vikings' recognition by winning a national contest.

"Based on my story and my football knowledge, the three NFL player judges selected me from a field of female football fans representing the other 29 teams. I was 'helmeted' the 'Ultimate Female Football Fan.' I was on numerous TV spots in my full Vikings gear, including European television stations." In addition, Battig was one of the first Viking Fan Club members, and she proudly wears a Minnesota Vikings tattoo.

Great victories are remembered and horrendous defeats must be endured as the Vikings' legacy continues. Brian Andrews, from North Port, Florida, became one of the Vikings faithful at the age of eight. He has an interesting way of dealing with devastating losses of the past. He owns the games on video and watches them over and over, each time hopeful that the results will be different! Andrews tries to remain confident that the endings are a mistake and will be corrected, but unfortunately, the results never change.

Andrews originally lived in New York; however, he would not settle for being a Giants fan. In fact, he was so against it that he took a Giants helmet and colored it with purple marker so it looked like a Vikings original. Of course, the Vikings horns had to be artistically drawn on the headgear's sides as well.

It must have been quite the helmet. It would be difficult to picture Frank Gifford or Sam Huff running around the field wearing one of those modified Giants helmets; the New York Giants football team would never have been the same!

Andrews developed his purple passion at a young age. "I did a report on Leif Ericson. I was just amazed by the exploration of the Vikings. My dad told me there was a football team with the name of Vikings. A fan for life was born," says Andrews. That was 38 years ago. "Living in Florida since 1973, I have had to feel the pain of Dolphins Super Bowl victories along with the Bucs championship." But that doesn't mean the memories are all bad, especially one Tampa Bay loss many years back in front of a cheering Bucs crowd.

"My fondest Vikings memory of a live game was at Tampa Stadium. Doug Williams scored a last-second touchdown to nearly tie the score. But the extra point was blocked by Wally Hilgenberg. Sixty-three thousand people were quiet except for the handful of Vikings fans. I will never forget the sounds of those cheers!" recalled Andrews.

Wally Hilgenberg was presented the game ball for the historic block that preserved the Vikings win. When he arrived home after the game, his wife and children were waiting for him in the driveway. They weren't there to congratulate him on his great play, however, but rather to inform him that his wonderful canine companion, Heidi, had been hit by a car and had died.

Heidi was an incredibly well trained and loving friend to Hilgenberg, and he occasionally brought her to Vikings practices. "She was so well trained I used to keep her in my locker while we were at practice," says Hilgenberg, "and she would always stay right there. Some of the guys would try to coax her out with donuts and other food, but she wouldn't move. Even after all these years, I can't look at that game ball and not think about Heidi being hit by the car on that day."

Along with the victories come losses. When the Dolphins beat the Vikings in the Super Bowl, a dismal loss for all the faithful, Brian Andrews wore his Vikings jacket to school the next day, deliberately showing everyone where his loyalties still lay.

As Andrews flies a Vikings flag proudly in front of his home each NFL season, he works diligently at another task. "Most importantly," Andrews proudly exclaims, "I am bringing up my three-and-a-half-year-old son to be a Vikings fan!"

The cold, wind, and snow are synonymous with the legacy of Minnesota Vikings football. When reminiscing, one can actually picture the Purple People Eaters lining up in the snow and ice-laden field of the old Metropolitan Stadium.

As he reflects upon his past, John Carter of North Liberty, Indiana, recalls playing football in the snow some 38 years ago, pretending to be one of the Viking greats. Living in Northern

Indiana, he should have been a Bears fan, but he wasn't; he was a Viking through and through.

"I didn't like the Bears," says Carter. "I liked the Vikings. I liked their uniforms and the fact that they played in such harsh conditions in Minnesota."

Carter loved the famed Purple People Eaters. He has always marveled at the fact that they all made the Pro Bowl. And what an accomplishment it was to have the Vikings' front four defensive men all recognized as the best in the league—and maybe the best ever.

One of Carter's greatest thrills occurred when Alan Page was named the NFL's Most Valuable Player. In the past, those kinds of accolades were reserved for offensive players, but Page's prowess could not be overlooked in 1971, as he was the first defensive player to win the award.

"Players like Alan Page shaped who I am today," Carter says. "Just watching them go all out on Sunday and seeing Joe Kapp and later Fran Tarkenton lead this team to glory was awesome."

It wasn't easy being a Vikings fan in Bears country, but he has survived it and remains loyal to the Purple. In the 1980s, Carter bought a satellite dish system, as he proudly explains, "just to watch my beloved Vikings." Now, with NFL Sunday Ticket, he gets to see the Vikings play every single Sunday.

"My wedding cake was a Vikings helmet in 2000," says Carter. "I love this team and I hope that all Vikings fans live long enough to see a world championship, because no fans in any sport are more deserving in my opinion. SKOL VIKINGS!"

In Northern Indiana, Carter professed his love for the Vikings uniforms. So did Robert Trainor of Lansing, Illinois. "I have been a Vikings fan for over 30 years. It's not easy living near Chicago. I fell for the purple uniforms in the fourth grade," says Trainor.

Among his great and historic Vikings memories, he recalls the "breath coming out of their mouths" as the Purple braved cold and horrific conditions going into battle at Met Stadium. The Vikings' fighting spirit captured Robert Trainor instantly.

Trainor proudly displays 17 different pieces of Viking fanfare in a small sitting room in his home. Lunch pails to clocks fill up the room. These items share the space with a 41-inch television specially purchased for Vikings games. When he can't get the games locally, Trainor, dressed in his treasured purple, sits in front of his computer and watches the play by play.

It is an unwritten rule that Robert Trainor should be left alone if the Vikings lose. "My wife thinks I take it to heart too much," says Trainor. "When watching the games, my heart rate speeds up to where it feels as if it could explode. The dogs won't stay in the same room with me and my wife prefers to go out because of the strong emotion I show."

"I am definitely known around town and at work as a Vikings fan," he continues. "Every year, I know the whole roster, not just the starters. I have pulled for Allen Rice, the Walker Lee Ashleys, the Reggie Rutlands, and the Matthew Hatchettes on the rosters."

If Robert Trainor had the only vote in a "Greatest Fan Contest," he would win. As he says, "I don't think I am the greatest fan, I know I am!" But there are others who might dispute the decision.

Aaron Polk was born in Minneapolis and now lives in Los Angeles, California. Many teams are located on the West Coast, but Polk is a diehard Vikings fan and has been since 1967.

"I watched the classic battles as the Purple People Eaters and the Fearsome Foursome of the Rams were forged into great defenses," says Polk. "Alan Page's speed ... Fran Tarkenton's uncanny elusiveness ... Joe Kapp's guile and grit ...Bobby Bryant's overachieving spirit ... these were but a few of the men who linked me with my hometown and the team which represented it for me far, far away."

"I battled single handedly all the local Rams fans and it was great," Polk says. "We rarely lost to them and the games were classics." But Polk doesn't have to tap far into his memory bank to come up with the most devastating loss for the Purple.

"Drew Pearson's catch is still etched in my mind ... the ball pinned against his hip after pushing off Nate Wright. Sure, the many Super Bowl losses hurt, but that one play epitomizes the pain that any true Vikings fan carries," says a disheartened Aaron Polk over 30 years later. Regardless of the occasional downs, though, he'll forever remain a fan.

It is in the far away location of Key West, Florida, that another great supporter, Larry Leopold, resides—a "live and die" Vikings fan since 1968.

"I wanted to be different," says Leopold. "My whole life I have had the Miami Dolphins shoved down my throat! I was beat up, bullied, and teased all through school. Yet as an adult now in my 40s, I am still their best fan!"

"I went to grade school and would go to the library and try to find articles about the Vikings," the avid fan continues. "I would go to magazine stores and cut out pictures. If I saw a picture that had to do with the Steelers, but a part of the picture had Wally Hilgenberg, No. 58, in it, the picture was cut out and put up on my wall."

"I'm tan, blonde, and 48 years old, and I want to be buried in purple. I'm at the end of the world here at Key West. I don't like other sports and am devoted to fishing, diving, and the Vikings," says Larry Leopold.

Leopold expresses concern over the fact that all sports talk revolved around the Dolphins as he grew up. "The first time I saw the Viking helmet with the horns on it, I knew this was my team forever. I used to come home in the heat of the day and watch the Vikings in the snow and it was special," Leopold says. "The Vikings are always in my heart, and I hope that one day we will pull it all off and win the Super Bowl."

Maybe Leopold's passion remains because the Purple have never achieved a championship. Maybe the crown, the ring, and the Super Bowl title are really what loom in the hearts of all those who love Vikings football. Maybe they are what keep the faith and passion alive. As Chuck Cutshall from Salinas, California, says, "I'll be waiting. Hopefully I will see them win the big one before I leave the earth!" But when Minnesota finally does win the big one, what then?

As the forever loyal Kim Lokken says, "Then we want another one!"

Depending on the circumstances, losing a bet as a diehard Vikings fan can be a disaster. And for Rebecca Mack Murphy of Columbia Heights, Minnesota, it was—she had to wear a Brett Favre jersey. It was painful, but in order to prevent the jersey from actually touching her skin, she wore a shirt under it, keeping the pain and humiliation to a minimum. The only benefit of the lost bet came when she told all of her friends that she had the opportunity to make the Packers quarterback look good for a change!

Vikings fans exist everywhere. It is hard to fully understand some connections, especially when an individual has never seen the Purple play a game in person or has never been in the state of Minnesota. Forever for the Purple, Phil Jordan is one of those fans.

"With the good times and the bad, my coworkers tell me it is amazing that I am such a diehard Vikings fan and have never seen them play and have never lived or visited Minnesota. Yes, Metropolitan Stadium in Bloomington, Minnesota in the winter. Below zero temperatures, frozen field, and no sideline heaters. Remember when they used to blow torch the field to thaw it out?" asks Jordan.

His favorite within the organization was Bud Grant. "Through it all, Bud Grant was stoic," remarks Jordan. "He still looks the same after all these years. Of all the coaches, I still miss Bud Grant the most!"

Purple losses were the toughest for Jordan, especially as a youngster. "I lived and breathed the Vikings growing up as a kid, and when they lost those four Super Bowls [against Kansas City, Miami, Oakland, and Pittsburgh] under Bud Grant, I had a major headache, and my parents used to always worry about how I was feeling," says Jordan. "I was so sick to my stomach that I didn't want to talk to anyone for days."

His loyalty and knowledge of the Vikings ran deep. He knew every player, and the more he learned about the franchise and those purple-clad athletes with horns on their heads, the more he loved them.

"I remember knowing all the players' names and positions," Jordan explains. "I liked the Purple People Eaters: Carl Eller, 81, Alan

Page, 88, Jim Marshall, 70. Who could forget Jim Marshall running the wrong way for a touchdown? I remember watching Lonnie Warwick, 59, Roy Winston, 60, and Wally Hilgenberg, 58. And of course Paul Krause, 22. On offense, I liked the tough and bowlegged Bill Brown, 30, and Osborn, 41. And who could forget Joe Kapp, 11? I used to try to hurdle people like Joe Kapp did when I eventually played high school football."

Phil Jordan's testimonial to the Vikings of old qualifies him as one of the team's great fans since the time he joined the ranks in 1961 upon the franchise's entry into the league. Says Jordan, "I grew up a fan of the Vikings even though I lived in New York when I started to follow them."

To this day, Jordan's devotion to the Purple is as strong as ever, regardless of the fact that he has never even stepped foot in Minnesota.

For some of the Purple faithful, there are ways to connect to the Vikings from long distances. You don't have to stand on the 50-yard line or any place else in the stadium. You don't even need to have a television in front of you or a radio within hearing distance.

Daniel Wessman doesn't let small problems get in his way of following the Vikings. "I was born a Viking," Wessman explains. "My story is upsetting when I think about it, but here it is. I was relocated to Texas when I was seven years old, but couldn't drop my Vikings even though I was in Cowboys country.

"I can't remember the exact year, but the Vikings were actually on TV for some reason and they were in a real battle at the end of the game. Dallas was the doubleheader game and they actually cut off the end of the Vikings game to announce the Dallas Cowboys game.

"I didn't miss a beat, grabbed the phone, and dialed my grandmother in Minnesota. She isn't the biggest fan in the world, but she knew how important it was to me. She gave me play-by-play

---

One-time Viking Jim Marshall (No. 70) has long been a fan favorite.
*Photo courtesy of the Minnesota Vikings*

action, even into overtime. When the game was final, I told her to apply for ESPN. I love my grandmother and I love my Vikings."

For some, rather unusual circumstances bring their loyalty to Vikingland. David Schuett of Central Wisconsin had a bad experience at his first football game as an eight-year-old at Lambeau Field that turned him away from the green and gold and toward the Purple. It seems that a famous Packer was rude to the young man, causing his loyalty to drift across the border.

"I have been the biggest Vikings fan since one miserable day at Lambeau Field," Schuett says. "It was a beautiful evening for a preseason game. I was sitting on the 50-yard line about 10 rows up with my sister and her boyfriend at the time and his grandfather. It was my first football game and I was excited. The game was just about ready to start when this large man smoking a cigar entered the same area I was in. He informed me very loudly that I was in his seat and he wanted me to move. He scared the daylights out of me and made me cry. He was big, ugly, and had hardly any teeth.

"When my sister noticed I was crying, she told him off and we later moved people way down on the other end so he could … sit down. I can still smell the horrible cigar coming from his face during the game. At halftime, people were coming up to this man to get his autograph. Turns out it was [a man who shall remain unnamed]. Little did this bozo know he would turn a little boy into the biggest Viking fan ever. Had it not been for [him], I would probably be just another Cheesehead grasping life on every one of No. 4's throws. Instead, I remain in Central Wisconsin just waiting for the day that we finally put a Super Bowl trophy into the case."

Purple passion captures many people in many different ways. In fact, the Vikings have been responsible for both ending and strengthening the relationships of one Watertown, New York, resident.

"I proposed to my wife at the Metrodome in 2002, when the Vikings hosted the Buffalo Bills," says Steve Payne, currently deployed in Afghanistan. "And in 1998, I dumped my girlfriend because she made fun of me when I cried because Gary Anderson missed his only field goal attempt all year at our most detrimental time—the NFC Championship against the 'dirty' Birds!"

Payne holds onto his Purple passion long distance. Though presently overseas, he has a Vikings game room in his New York apartment and a Darrin Sharper jersey proudly hanging above his Vikings body pillow. In his wallet, he carries the newspaper clipping announcing Cris Carter's retirement. Born in Little Falls, Minnesota, Steve truly believes he is "one of the greatest Viking fans who ever lived." And he may be.

Most people who love sports grab hold of the local franchise based in their hometown. This is pretty common. If you live in Cincinnati, your team is the Bengals. If you grew up in Detroit and still live in Motor City, you probably root for the Lions. If your residence is in Oakland, California, more than likely you have become a Raider fan.

But some go against the common thread. Purple blood runs through their veins and, regardless of location, they have no other choice but to cheer for the men in purple apparel.

"It is tough to be a lifelong Vikings fan from deep in enemy territory ... in my case, Dallas, Texas. But the alternative is to become a fan of the locals, and my blood is eternally purple," says Christopher Allen. "I became a Vikings fan in Kentucky, of all places. With no 'local' NFC team, the CBS affiliate was free to run whichever NFL game it choose each Sunday ... so we consistently got either the Cowboys, the Vikings, or Rams games because those were the best teams then.

"EVERYBODY was already a Cowboys fan [there was something irritating about 'America's team' even then] and the Rams always played late games, by which time my brothers were already outside emulating our gridiron heroes with the neighbor kids. I was a small kid ... and I was hooked when I saw Fran Tarkenton—who looked impossibly small compared to the linemen chasing him even then—running 30 yards back, then 50 yards across the line of scrimmage to overcome those enormous opponents and complete a five-yard pass to a back. I loved that!"

"My career brought me to Cowboys land, but I never shook my purple loyalty," continues Allen. "My fondest memory is being invited as a charter member of the fan club to be on the field for the season opener in 1998, where I held the Viking Fan Club flag for Texas as the players ran onto the field.

"Purple I am, purple I always will be ... until that long-cherished Super Bowl championship is finally achieved and beyond!"

Jill Lovig follows the Vikings from Iowa and would likely not be any more of a fan if she lived across from the Metrodome. "My life is the Vikings," she says. "Everything I own is the Vikings. ... My dad is a fan and I think it comes from the blood, because my blood is purple. I have three girls and they are Vikings fans too. We hate the Packers!"

Loving the Vikings is always an important pronouncement to make, but hating the Packers at the same time is something very, very special!

Fans come in all shapes and sizes. They come in all colors and in both sexes. They all have their own special ways of ensuring that their loyalties are properly presented. And most are very different from one another.

Rob Jussila of Northern Ontario played defensive end in high school during the 1970s and became hooked on the Vikings.

"I used to draw the No. 81 on my sweater and used the marker to write 'Eller' on the back of the jersey. The only channel that carried any of the NFL games was a local French channel, so I spent most Sundays watching the Vikes in French, even though I didn't understand a word they were saying ... except 'touché,' which the Vikings did a lot in those days."

Rob says that his picture in the high school yearbook proclaims, "One of my aspirations in life was to play defensive end for the Vikes. I will be a Vikings fan for life and hopefully they will win a Super Bowl sometime during the remaining years, which will allow me to RIP."

Minnesota-born Rich Harthan would also rest in peace. As he passionately says, "The Vikes will win the Super Bowl before I die!"

If "biggest fan" applications could only be accepted from those who had to make their pronouncements in one short sentence, Tom Pietrosimone from West Haven, Connecticut, would definitely be in the running. He would proudly announce he has a Vikings tattoo and a "Dalmatian named Dozier." Pietrosimone has followed his team in purple for many years and has "Vikings football flowing through my blood." If he is not the Vikings' biggest fan, he likely ranks near the top.

Bob Bevard is a motivational speaker who travels extensively. "The Vikes are my team, always—no matter their record, no matter that I live 1,200 miles south of the Twin Cities."

For many years, his home has been San Antonio, Texas, yet the Purple remain his team. "I was raised in Minneapolis and I still remember with a grimace … the Pearson catch which gave the win to the Cowboys. Cowboys fans thought it was a great catch. Vikes fans thought it was pass interference. An easy call. A call that wasn't made," says Bevard.

"I still HATE the Cowboys and take great delight in cheering for the opposing team—any opposing team," he professes. While traveling, it has become a high priority for Bevard to "try to find some location that has the Vikes game and cheer for the Purple People Eaters!"

Hawaii has also been home to one of the true Vikings' faithful for the past 37 years. Bert Morikuni fell in love with the Purple at the age of six in 1969. Anyone can understand. It was the Vikings-Rams playoff game at the old Met Stadium that cemented his loyalty forever. If ever a game could bring lasting passion, that one would be it—one of the best ever.

"I remember the Vikings clinching the victory with a safety of the Rams' Roman Gabriel. Oh, those Purple People Eaters. Since that 1969 Vikings-Rams game until now I've been a Vikings diehard fan," says Morikuni.

In his 37 years loving the Men of Purple, Morikuni has seen it all—many lows and many highs. "I've witnessed all the down moments in Vikings history," says Morikuni. "The four Super Bowl losses, the Drew Pearson 'Hail Mary' offensive pass interference TD to knock us out of the playoffs, the Tony Dorsett 99-yard TD run ... the Washington Redskins-Vikings NFC Championship game in which Wade Wilson almost got the TD pass to Darrin Nelson that would have tied the game ... and the most painful one of them all—the 1998 NFC Championship game between the Atlanta Falcons and the Vikings. ... Incredible."

Franchise highs existed as well, and Bert Morikuni bled purple during those great victories. Explains Morikuni, "I've also witnessed all the up moments in Vikings history: the Tommy Kramer to Ahmad Rashad 'Hail Mary' to win the Central Division Championship, Fran 'The Man' Tarkenton, the Purple People Eaters, Chuck Foreman, Randy 'Super Freak' Moss, Bud Grant, Metropolitan Stadium in Bloomington, Minnesota. The '70s went and the Vikings dominated the Central Division."

"The most memorable Viking play to me was Nate Allen blocking Tom Dempsey's field goal attempt and Bobby Bryant picking it up and running 90 yards for a touchdown in which the Vikings beat the Rams in the NFC Championship to advance to the Super Bowl. I've been following Vikings football from Hawaii," says Morikuni, surely qualifying as a lifetime fan.

One's passions often carry over into many other parts of life. For Meshell Herrick, being a Vikings fan has had a major impact on home decorating. "We have graduated our Purple home decorating from a bathroom to the entryway of our home to an office and finally to an entertainment room. We recently purchased a house and have a plan for the new entertainment room. It will have Astroturf, purple walls, and it will be decked out with autographs of young and old," says Herrick.

While living in Germany for two and a half years, Herrick had to watch games in the wee hours of the morning when they were televised live. She also got her Vikings fix by going to NFL Europe games and making connections with players who wear purple back in the States.

One of her all-time biggest thrills came with a 30th birthday gift from her husband while she was still in Germany. He surprised her with a round-trip ticket to Minneapolis to see the Packers play the

Vikings. Her husband stayed in Germany to watch their four children while Herrick lived her dream.

After the game, some of the Vikings players found out how far she had traveled and accommodated her with many wonderful pictures—a great memory for a great fan!

Herrick's family has also attended a great many Vikings road games since returning to the States. Because of some medical issues with her son, Carter, game attendance has not been as regular. But watching the Vikings' training camp at Mankato while living in a tent for several days remains a family tradition.

"We were at Korey Stringer's last practice," says Herrick. "We took photos that day. Just the season before I received a black and white of Korey autographed to me. I do not go to a game without a '77' on my body somewhere!

"This was a huge turning point in my Viking fandom. The players became people just like me. They have families and football is their job. What they do on the field is gifted and unfathomable for most people to believe ever possible."

Herrick has some great memories, but more are on the horizon. "I still have places I'd love to go with the Vikings. I would love to be at Lambeau to cheer on the Purple! Someday I will live, breathe, and cheer purple in Wisconsin!" she exclaims. "I will see the day the Vikings make it to the Super Bowl and win! In my mind, it will happen every year! We have an equal shot at it every year! Yet, before I die … my dream … [is] to sing the National Anthem at a Vikings home game. Then, I can be placed in the ranks of one of the HUGEST Viking fans ever! Purple Pride lives in the heart of the diehard fan!!!"

All the way from Hephzibah, Georgia, Wendell Singleton sings the praises of the Men who wear the Purple. "Since the years of Tarkenton, Alan Page, Marshall, Carl Eller, and Chuck Foreman, I've been a Purple People Eater. The year … when Fran Tarkenton's dad had his heart attack because the Dallas Cowboys and the referee cheated, I too almost had one. Since then I have hated the Cowboys and I am living for the day we get our revenge," says Singleton.

"My whole family—grandmother included—were loyal fans to Bud Grant and the Vikings. When I die, I will bleed purple blood! If I could walk the sidelines during game days, I know the Vikings would be a better team right now, because I know how a Viking is supposed to play," Singleton explains. "They need to adapt the real attitude of a true Viking from the days of the '70s and '80s and stir in some Bud Grant and I promise you a true Vikings fan could die in peace."

If an honor was to be given out to the greatest Viking fan ever and the trophy went to Windell Singleton, it would, as he says, "be the lost Super Bowl to me."

Long oratories and firsthand examples are not needed to explain Vancouver, British Colombia, native Steve McLaren's love of the Minnesota Vikings. He puts it quite simply. "I was 10 years old when I first remembered the Purple People Eaters ... I'm from Vancouver, BC, and the closest team to me is Seattle, but when the Vikes come there, you'll know who I'm cheering for!"

In Las Vegas, many things can be done to keep busy, but not when the Vikings are playing. As one of the Purple faithful, James Coon knows this. Traveling to out of town games and cheering on the team from home are all just a part of it. "Shaving the hair off his chest and back" prepares him for game day, since painting the body purple comes with the territory of being a loyal Vikings fan.

Cheryl Billingsley from New Jersey would be the Vikings' No. 1 fan of all time if she were doing the voting and represented the only vote. She truly believes she should be an Eagles fan, but followed her Eagles players to the land of the Purple. She now cherishes all those who wear the color.

She once ran down Cris Carter at a concert and again tracked him down when the Vikes later visited the Eagles. He singled out the passionate, resilient fan in a crowd and rewarded her with a great picture, proving Billingsley to be one of the Vikings' greatest fans.

Becoming a great Vikings fan is the tradition for the Mascarenas family of Avondale, Arizona, home of Viking great Randall McDaniel. "In our town, our name is synonymous with the Vikings," says Rene Mascarenas. "My dad used to tell me stories of watching

Joe Kapp, Carl Eller, Chuck Foreman, Sammy White, and Ahmad Rashad."

People in the area think the family is "crazy" according to Mascarenas, because "we live 1835.36 miles away." But this is why they have to root for the Vikings "harder, and more passionately." And the reality is, how could someone living down the block from Randall McDaniel not be a Vikings fan? One of the greatest players in team history, he was perhaps the best offensive guard to ever play the game!

Passion for the Purple ends with "Viking Joe" from Fayettevelle, North Carolina. "I was a fan of the Vikings movies with the long ships as they sailed the seas," says Joseph Minyon. It started in 1969 when Minyon was looking for something to identify with and has lasted throughout his world travels in the Air Force. "I made my first trip to Minnesota and attended the game against Detroit. I was one of the screaming fans on their feet in the fourth quarter when we caused a John Kitna fumble and scored. I felt that was my touchdown, as I was on the 200 level and could not hear from all the noise. So I am positive that the Lions never heard a thing, and that caused the fumble."

"So, for 37 years, I have said, 'GO VIKES!!!'" says Fayetteville's Viking Joe. "I know our day is coming soon to return to the Super Bowl and I intend to be there to finally bring home the prize."

Supporters of the Men who wear the Purple are not just local, but come from all parts of the region, the United States, and the world. "Our, us, we, together, collectively" are all words signifying the fans and their beloved Purple as one. Winning is not just done by the players and losing is not just endured by those in uniform—PURPLE PASSION is unified and united, a connection that forever remains in the heart.

# 8

# PURPLE HONOR, PURPLE FAME

GLORY, STARDOM, DIGNITY, DISTINCTION, AND PRESTIGE—all are words that come with deep respect. They connect to something that is earned, not merely given. Received from others and unable to be attributed to one's self, respect is a credit to that individual who has attained recognition for accomplishments set apart from others. It is a status brought about by performance that stands out from the usual and routine. Respect means honor and it means fame. And for those who achieved it wearing purple, it became PURPLE HONOR AND PURPLE FAME.

Certain former members of the Minnesota Vikings football team have achieved that reverence. Election to the Pro Football Hall of Fame in Canton, Ohio, or induction into the Vikings' Ring of Honor comes with the highest of adulation and is shared by few.

Overall, seven former Vikings have been elected into the Pro Football Hall of Fame and 15 have been inducted into the Ring of Honor.

Other individuals who coached or very briefly played for the Vikings and have been elected to the Pro Football Hall of Fame are: Hugh McElhenny, halfback from 1961 to 1962; Norm Van Brocklin, head coach from 1961 to 1966; Jim Langer, center from 1980 to 1981; Jan Stenerud, kicker from 1984 to 1985; Dave Casper, tight end in 1983; and Warren Moon, quarterback from 1994 to 1996.

Each made great contributions to the Purple and has achieved monumental accomplishments during their storied careers.

When looking at a professional football organization such as the Minnesota Vikings, who have been in operation for four and a half decades, one quickly realizes that thousands of players and coaches have worn the purple apparel.

To be selected out of that group of highly skilled and well-conditioned athletes and ordained into the Minnesota Vikings Ring of Honor is something special. As stated in the *Vikings 2006 Official Team Guide,* "The Ring of Honor recognizes Viking legends for their contributions to the success of the team on and off the field. Members of the Ring of Honor are recognized with a banner on the façade of the Metrodome's upper deck, forever living in Vikings lore."

Selection to Vikings fame is a lasting tribute to the great men who have worn the purple with distinction. But some have even gone beyond this credit by way of their extraordinary performances and have been elected to the Pro Football Hall of Fame, the highest attainable honor. To be enshrined in Canton, Ohio, is to reach the pinnacle of success in professional football.

Former Packer great and Hall of Fame member Ray Nitschke was once credited for saying to new inductees, "You can't be cut, waived, or traded from this team; you are a lifetime member."

## FRAN TARKENTON
### MINNESOTA VIKINGS RING OF HONOR AND
### PRO FOOTBALL HALL OF FAME MEMBER

He was significant in making every game he ever played in interesting from start to finish. Fran Tarkenton played for the Vikings from 1961 to 1966 and then returned to the Purple from 1972 to 1978. He was the premier player in a trade between the Vikings and New York Giants in 1967 and in his return to the Purple in 1972.

Few players reach stardom in a career. Even fewer reach the status in their very first game and are able to keep it throughout an illustrious career. Fran Tarkenton did just that.

As a third-round draft pick in 1961 out of the University of Georgia, Tarkenton came off the bench in the Minnesota Vikings' first game and helped crush the Chicago Bears 37-13. "Helped" is probably an understatement, considering he threw for four touchdown passes in his Purple debut.

He led the Vikings to three Super Bowls and was a four-time NFL All-Pro at quarterback. He played in nine Pro Bowl games, was elected into the Pro Football Hall of Fame on August 2, 1986, and inducted into the Ring of Honor on September 9, 1998.

Despite all the great recognitions bestowed upon him, Tarkenton is most known in Minnesota Vikings lore as the man who could bring passion and fervor to the game in the most exciting fashion. The "Scrambler," as he was lovingly called by the faithful, brought many a fan to his feet as he ran for his life, while men of steel and fierceness hunted him down. And all too often, after the race across the field of play was over, did the athlete, adorned in purple, destroy the chasers' spirits by one sweeping motion of his right arm or the forward dancing of his body and legs. He may have worn No. 10 on the field, but Fran Tarkenton was No. 1 in the fans' hearts.

# ALAN PAGE
## MINNESOTA VIKINGS RING OF HONOR AND PRO FOOTBALL HALL OF FAME MEMBER

He came out of the University of Notre Dame as a first-round pick of the Vikings in 1967. He played in 236 straight games in his career and four Super Bowls for Minnesota from 1967 to 1978.

In 1971, he was the first defensive player to be named the NFL's Most Valuable Player. Number 88 was a great athlete throughout his career and unstoppable on his greatest days.

He was a terrific player and one of the famed Purple People Eaters. He recorded 148.5 sacks and recovered 23 opponents'

Alan Page (No. 88) is not only a member of the Pro Football Hall of Fame, but he also continues to effect change off the playing field.

*Photo courtesy of the Minnesota Vikings*

fumbles. But most incredible, Alan Page blocked 28 kicks. An astonishing number, some entire football teams don't block that many kicks in decades.

To Page, the records are certainly important, but his real goal was to be remembered for what he has accomplished off the field.

He is a Supreme Court Justice and established the Page Education Foundation, which helps generate educational pursuits for the underprivileged—something close and most valuable to his being.

He was one of the greatest players ever to wear the purple. Page was one of the fastest and quickest defensive linemen to play the game and brought constant, immense joy to the faithful who watched him perform each Sunday.

Alan Page was elected into the Pro Football Hall of Fame on June 30, 1998, and inducted into the Minnesota Vikings Ring of Honor on September 20, 1998.

# JIM FINKS
## MINNESOTA VIKINGS RING OF HONOR AND PRO FOOTBALL HALL OF FAME MEMBER

Jim Finks was truly a legend in Vikings history. He was a great administrator and negotiator, and recognized throughout the league as a top judge of player talent. Most who worked for Jim Finks held him in high esteem.

He treated people with dignity and respect. Finks played professional football for the Pittsburgh Steelers and was an administrator in the Canadian Football League prior to becoming Minnesota's general manager and administrator. He was instrumental in signing many famed Viking players and responsible for bringing Bud Grant to the Vikings from the Canadian Football League. Finks was also a key ingredient in two Viking Super Bowl appearances.

The general manager was inducted into the Pro Football Hall of Fame on July 29, 1995, and into the Ring of Honor on October 18, 1998.

# BUD GRANT
## MINNESOTA VIKINGS RING OF HONOR AND PRO FOOTBALL HALL OF FAME MEMBER

Harry Peter "Bud" Grant was the face of the franchise for four decades. And, though he has not coached for over 20 years, many still associate Bud Grant with the team as the franchise's unspoken leader.

It has been said that his personality and stoic sideline demeanor are what kept the organization together. Things would always be OK while Grant was in charge. He was loved by the faithful and greatly respected by those who worked and played for him. He was a magnificent leader and a great football coach. Mostly, however, he was an exceptional judge of character and people in general.

Bud Grant, who was elected to the Pro Football Hall of Fame on July 30, 1994, and into the Ring of Honor on November 8, 1998, has become an area icon, symbolic of all that's been right in the Minnesota Vikings organization for over 40 years.

Grant had something to give and did so smoothly, professionally, and with little fan fare. Few have ever been able to obtain the presence he possesses.

The longtime head coach won numerous football games with the Vikings, and led them to four Super Bowl appearances and 11 divisional championships. He won 158 regular-season games in his tenure and remains a part of the franchise to this day.

## PAUL KRAUSE
### MINNESOTA VIKINGS RING OF HONOR AND PRO FOOTBALL HALL OF FAME MEMBER

"He was a great athlete and a great basketball and football player. He had the greatest pair of hands of anyone I have ever seen," said Jerry Burns. "No one ever played the safety position better."

Recorded in the books are 81 interceptions, an unbelievable total. This entry's owner played for the Vikings from 1968 to 1979, starting at safety in four Super Bowls and playing in eight pro bowls. While Fran Tarkenton shined as a rookie, so did he. Twelve interceptions led the league that year, and the name next to this phenomenal number was Paul Krause.

Krause was like a graceful center fielder who patrolled the Minnesota Vikings' outfield. The field general on defense, he was successful in keeping the game in front of him. He was also the holder on field goals and extra points, another tribute to his great hands and athletic ability.

No. 22, Paul Krause, was elected to the Pro Football Hall of Fame on August 1, 1998, and inducted into the Ring of Honor on November 15, 1998.

# FRED ZAMBERLETTI
## MINNESOTA VIKINGS RING OF HONOR

Fred Zamberletti is the franchise's cornerstone and a lifelong mentor to the organization. In the past 46 years, he has never missed a game with the Vikings.

"I have known Fred Zamberletti most of my life, and he is the most respected trainer. There is no better trainer than Fred," says Jerry Burns, who began working with Zamberletti at Iowa over four decades ago. Bill McGrane calls him "the anchor for the players to hold onto."

Since the inception of the Minnesota Vikings franchise in 1961, the name Fred Zamberletti has stood for leader, mentor, friend, advisee, and "voice of reason." He has modeled the terms credibility, honesty, and integrity.

He was named Professional Athletic Trainer of the Year in 1986 and, in 1996, was honored along with the rest of his colleagues as part of the NFL Athletic Training Staff of the Year.

When people are asked to describe Fred Zamberletti, their comments are heartfelt. The man is loved and respected for his work, his friendship, and his glorious heart.

When Fred Zamberletti is asked to describe Fred Zamberletti, he replies, "I was lucky. I have great respect for the people I grew up with—coal miners and immigrants. I am very lucky for the friends that I have had in my life."

When speaking of his great career and role with the Vikings through the years, Zamberletti replies, "I have received more than I have ever given."

Fred Zamberletti has been a fixture in the Vikings organization since the team's origination in 1961. *Photo courtesy of the Minnesota Vikings*

Fred Zamberletti was inducted into the Minnesota Vikings Ring of Honor on December 20, 1998. Sports legends are most often associated with athletic prowess. But this example of legendary status purely relates to a man who comes to work every day and does his job in a way that leaves an indelible imprint upon all those who have known and associated with him. He is a man of the greatest of esteem.

# JIM MARSHALL
## MINNESOTA VIKINGS RING OF HONOR

When purple jerseys are on display, when Minnesota takes the field, and when the Vikings are brought up on radio, television, or in idle conversation, the image of Jim Marshall, No. 70, materializes. It has always been, or, better said, must always be that way.

Marshall played in 282 consecutive games and started in 270 of them. Hurt, sick, or worn out, the athlete was effective for 20 seasons. He had 29 fumble recoveries, and played in two Pro Bowls and four Super Bowls. Jim Marshall was a great player and fan favorite for two decades.

"He was the greatest athlete to ever play for the Vikings," says Fred Zamberletti. "He could have been a decathlete. He had a tremendous arsenal of stamina and made great sacrifices for the Vikings. I'd like to find a couple more like him today."

Former teammate Jim Lindsey says, "I loved Jim Marshall. There was no player more resilient and no more of a complete player."

Jim Marshall was inducted into the Minnesota Vikings Ring of Honor on November 28, 1999. Although he is not a member of the Pro Football Hall of Fame, he should be. Marshall played for 20 years without ever missing a game. While his longevity alone is incredible, he was also Minnesota's leader and a skilled football player.

Sunday after Sunday, he fought athletes' toughest wars. When the history of the Purple is discussed, Jim Marshall comes to the conversation's forefront. In the eyes of those who watched him, coached him, and played with or against him, Jim Marshall is in the Pro Football Hall of Fame—it just isn't official yet.

# RON YARY
## MINNESOTA VIKINGS RING OF HONOR AND
## PRO FOOTBALL HALL OF FAME

The Vikings selected Ron Yary as the first offensive lineman in the history of the league to be taken first in the NFL Draft. The following season, he started at right tackle for the Vikings and stayed there forever. At least, it seemed like that.

One of the most dominating players ever to play in the league, he was a fixture in the position. Throughout 15 seasons of play, he was named All-Pro and All-NFC six and eight consecutive years, respectively, and played in seven Pro Bowls and four Super Bowls.

Fred Zamberletti calls Ron Yary unique. "He was a strong, tough competitor—a great player." Yary set the tone for offensive linemen. He had a monumental work ethic, playing the game with great inspiration and fortitude. Coaches never worried about their ferocious right tackle as he was put into the lineup every game.

Ron Yary was elected to the Pro Football Hall of Fame on August 4, 2001, and inducted into the Minnesota Vikings Ring of Honor on September 9, 2001.

## KOREY STRINGER
### MINNESOTA VIKINGS RING OF HONOR

Korey Stringer was a massive tackle out of Ohio State University, chosen by the Vikings as the 24th pick in the 1995 NFL Draft.

He started the second game of his rookie season at right tackle and remained in the position for six seasons. Possessing great athletic ability at 6-foot-5 and 335 pounds, Stringer was an anchor on the right side of the Vikings' line.

In addition to being an outstanding football player, Stringer was a "great guy." He was involved in many community activities and had a special place in his heart for young people. At the age of 27, Korey Stringer died suddenly at training camp during the 2001 season. He was inducted into the Minnesota Vikings Ring of Honor November 19, 2001.

# MICK TINGELHOFF
## MINNESOTA VIKINGS RING OF HONOR

Mick Tingelhoff came out of the University of Nebraska as a free agent. He wasn't drafted, but played for the Minnesota Vikings for 17 seasons. Tingelhoff started every game, a total of 240 straight, while with the Vikings.

He was named to the All-Pro Team seven consecutive years and played in six Pro Bowls. In 1969, the NFL's top blocker was named to the 1,000 Yard Club. Tingelhoff was a great player and teammate.

Perhaps the best center to ever play the game, he was also the long snapper on punts, field goals, and extra points—a role not seen in professional football today.

Most players feel it is a travesty that Mick Tingelhoff is not in the Pro Football Hall of Fame. Jim Lindsey is one of them. "It's not in the record books, but if they ever recorded how many tackles Mick made covering punts and on interceptions, the numbers would be staggering," Lindsey says. "I don't think he ever made a bad snap. No one really knows how complete a player he was."

Tingelhoff was associated with the Vikings and honored for his play for so many years that it seemed unusual once he was no longer out there on Sundays in the fall. Mick Tingelhoff was elected into the Minnesota Vikings Ring of Honor November 25, 2001.

Great centers need a place to rest. A bust of Tingelhoff was made in the 17 years he anchored the Minnesota Vikings' offensive line and is ready to rest in its proper place. A special space is set aside for Mick Tingelhoff in the Pro Football Hall of Fame in Canton, Ohio. He belongs and will hopefully be there soon.

# CARL ELLER
## MINNESOTA VIKINGS RING OF HONOR AND PRO FOOTBALL HALL OF FAME MEMBER

In Minnesota, Carl Eller has been a name synonymous with "great football player" since he set foot on the University of Minnesota campus in 1960. He played for the Golden Gophers from

1961 to 1963 and was drafted by the Minnesota Vikings in 1964 with the sixth overall pick. He was an All-American and an All-Pro.

He played in 209 Vikings games and started in 201of them. He played in six Pro Bowls and four Super Bowls.

A great athlete and a magnificent player, Carl Eller was a master at his position and a dominating defensive end with 130 sacks, including at least one in eight consecutive games.

No. 81 lit up the television screens with his terrific play and set stadiums and crowds on fire with his passion. He was a magnificent force and crowd pleaser in a violent game for 16 NFL seasons.

Carl Eller was elected into the Pro Football Hall of Fame on August 8, 2004, and inducted into the Minnesota Vikings Ring of Honor on November 10, 2002.

## CRIS CARTER
### MINNESOTA VIKINGS RING OF HONOR

Cris Carter will go down in NFL history as one of the greatest receivers to ever play the game. In 16 seasons, he started 177 as a Viking. He was named to the All-Pro Team four times and played in eight straight Pro Bowls.

While with the Vikings, Carter caught at least one pass in 111 straight games. The athlete was named part of the 1990's Team of the Decade. Cris was named recipient of the Byron "Whizzer" White Award by the NFL Players Association and the Walter Payton "Man of the Year" Award in 1999, which he received at the 2000 Super Bowl.

He was a steady pass receiver and a tremendous offensive "controlling-type player." A "ball collector" when it came time to move the chains, he made some of the greatest catches of all time to take control of games.

Center Mick Tingelhoff (No. 53) protects fellow Viking Joe Kapp.
*Photo courtesy of the Minnesota Vikings*

Cris Carter was inducted into the Minnesota Vikings Ring of Honor on September 14, 2003. A place has been reserved for Cris Carter in Canton, Ohio, as one of the greatest receivers to ever play the game.

## BILL BROWN
### MINNESOTA VIKINGS RING OF HONOR

The Chicago Bears traded Bill Brown to Minnesota in 1962. A University of Illinois alum, he played for the Vikings from 1962 to 1974. He was a bone-crushing, hard-hitting fullback who could block, run, and catch passes with great prowess.

He was a dominating athlete who played in three Super Bowls for the Vikings and four Pro Bowls. His bruising style of play and fearless attitude made him a fan favorite.

Jim Lindsey played with Bill Brown and loved his passion for the game. "Bill Brown loved football more than anyone you would ever want to meet," says Lindsey.

Bill Brown was inducted into the Minnesota Vikings Ring of Honor on September 26, 2004.

Says Jerry Burns, "He was a team player, and the best blocking full back and the best pass receiving full back of his time."

## JERRY BURNS
### MINNESOTA VIKINGS RING OF HONOR

Jerry Burns was Minnesota Vikings offensive coordinator from 1968 to 1985 and head coach from 1986 to 1991. As the offensive coordinator for the Vikings, he assisted the Vikings to four Super Bowls and 11 divisional titles.

Burns was an offensive genius. Other teams asked him to assist as a consultant many times early in his career.

He was head coach at Iowa from 1961 to 1965 and the Green Bay Packers defensive backs coach throughout their Super Bowl winning seasons in 1966 and 1967.

Jerry Burns is one of the most beloved of all Vikings. Players and fans revere him, saying, "Burnsie, what a great guy!"

Jerry Burns was inducted into the Minnesota Vikings Ring of Honor on November 6, 2005.

## RANDALL MCDANIEL
### MINNESOTA VIKINGS RING OF HONOR

Randall McDaniel played 12 seasons for the Minnesota Vikings from 1988 to 1999. He was named as a Pro Bowl selection 12 times and competed on playoff teams 11 times.

McDaniel was an intelligent, dominating offensive lineman. As a Viking, he started 170 consecutive games—fourth on Minnesota's all-time list. Randall McDaniel simply came to work and did his job every day with little fan fare. He just happened to do it better than most who have played the game of professional football.

The ultimate team player, McDaniel was well liked and an anchor in the line. He was such a regular at the Pro Bowl that his name became almost automatic in the selection process. He may have been one of the best—if not the very best—offensive guards to ever play the game.

Randall McDaniel was inducted into the Minnesota Vikings Ring of Honor on December 17, 2006. His bust will soon be cast and placed in Canton, Ohio, in the Pro Football Hall of Fame. Somewhere in the inscription will also rest the words "maybe the best ever."

The Professional Football Hall of Fame and the Minnesota Vikings Ring of Honor are awards of recognition honoring the best to ever play the game. What makes the above list so special? They were all Men of Purple.

# 9

# PURPLE COACHES

OVER THE PAST FOUR AND A HALF DECADES, millions have, in devoted fashion, supported a group of athletes in purple apparel with horns on the sides of their heads. These steadfast faithful have trudged through the wind, sleet, and snow in the most challenging of weather conditions to sit at times in pure, frigid misery at the old Metropolitan Stadium in Bloomington, Minnesota—all in hopes of cheering the Minnesota Vikings to victory.

From 1961 to 1982, this was the domicile of the Men who wore the Purple. And the passionate joy felt by loyal followers over great triumphs meant just as much as the horrific sadness that dampened and chilled the surroundings in painful and historic defeats. Forever the faithful, they came through the turnstiles to watch and applaud in support of the great Viking teams throughout the decades.

And countless more listened to the radio and watched on television as the beloved Purple roamed the frozen field of their Bloomington home and later basked in the Metrodome's warmth in downtown Minneapolis.

As the unwavering, allegiant millions watched, thousands played. They wore all the numbers and they played at all of the positions. Big and small, fast and strong, they all performed their profession wearing those treasured purple uniforms.

Some stayed for a few days, some for a few weeks or months, and some for years. Some were drafted, some came from other teams, and some arrived on their own. They came from colleges, other franchises, and across the northern border. Once here, however, their bond became common. They had horns on their helmets and they all wore purple—they were Minnesota Vikings.

For 46 seasons in the fall, millions of hearty, faithful fans have watched and cheered for the thousands who've played. And through all the glorious years, these great athletes have been led onto the fields of play by only seven. In the celebrated and magnificent history of Viking football, only seven men have held the distinguished title of head coach.

Seven men. For thousands of players and millions of fans, seven have led the Purple over 46 seasons. They were named Norm Van Brocklin, Bud Grant, Les Steckel, Jerry Burns, Dennis Green, Mike Tice, and Brad Childress. They were the head coaches of the Minnesota Vikings.

First was The Dutchman, Norm Van Brocklin. He was a great player with fierce passion and desire for the game, and an unmatched, relentless pursuit for ultimate victory.

Already a household name, he brought with him a legendary status as a player. He was a future Hall of Famer and an inspirational leader, as long as the scoreboard read in favor of the Vikings. What more could an upstart franchise in the NFL ask for but a man like Norm Van Brocklin to lead the charge?

Some say The Dutchman was tough to play for, while others recognize his ferocious passion for winning and inability to accept losses. He believed everyone should play the game with the passionate desire and the same greatness he once did. Few could, and when they didn't meet his standards, it was difficult for him to understand or accept.

Van Brocklin was a great athlete who truly understood the game. He was an offensive genius, and few could match his knowledge and passion. His wisdom made it an appealing and sometimes easy task to dissect defenses in the NFL. As a player, Van Brocklin had entered a special "circle of greatness," and very few ever enjoyed the athletic ability and prowess to join him there.

Six years went by under the leadership of Van Brocklin before Bud Grant arrived on the scene as the second head coach of the Minnesota Vikings. For 17 years, and later one more, he led the Purple to great heights with unforgettable seasons and championships.

Bud cemented in place the team's foundation and, even in the toughest of times, was the glue holding it all together. His fan base and support were never in question. He was Bud Grant, former Minnesota Gopher great and head coach of the Purple. He belonged.

The faithful and the players both trusted him, and, even after a horrendous or disappointing loss, everyone knew things would still be all right; Bud was in charge.

After Grant's retirement in 1984, a young assistant coach took over the Vikings. His name was Les Steckel. As has been written many times of the Steckel legacy, standing alone, his name denotes failure among the elite group of people known as head coaches in the NFL.

Les Steckel, by his own admission, should not have taken the job as head coach of the Minnesota Vikings. He was too young and inexperienced. He was not ready and he is the first to admit it.

There is an attractive and honorable attribute to the personality of Les Steckel. He is not afraid to admit or speak about his career failures and their effects on him. In many ways, the disappointment has reflected positively upon his life and that of others.

In his book *One Yard Short*, released this past year, Steckel says, "I expect to be the first inductee into the pink slip Hall of Fame." He is realistic about his failure and unashamed of seven other football firings that have occurred along his trail of coaching memories in a remarkable career.

Steckel has been a keynote speaker for college football coaches many times over the years at various meetings and conferences. He routinely poses the following question to the several thousand coaches in attendance: "How many of you have been fired in your career in coaching?" This generally results in the raising of numerous hands. He then asks, "How many of you have been fired twice in your career?"

Fewer hands are raised, but several do acknowledge a second dismissal. In response to the third question, "How many of you have been fired three times?" he has never seen a hand go up.

Assuming the logic if someone is willing to admit being fired twice, it is likely they would also admit if removed a third time. Les Steckel was fired from coaching positions a total of eight times. True, some of the decisions were based upon head coaches being fired and his being let go as an assistant coach; however, paycheck-wise, "fired" would be an accurate way to portray the circumstances of his departure.

Steckel is realistic about his career, admits failure and speaks of it as a blessing in his life, and truly accepts what has happened as a testing of his resolve. The path forward has made him a better and stronger person.

In *One Yard Short*, he apologizes to his players and coaches for the difficult 1984 season when he was the Vikings' head coach: "To this day, I offer my deepest apologies to the players and coaches who were bruised during my learning experience." And he is very sincere about it. When asked if he should have been fired after the dreadful 3-13 season, Steckel replied, "Absolutely!"

After his firing, Les remarked to his wife, "It is better for us to go through this difficult time so that others like Jerry Burns and John Michels can get their lives back together." He was extremely distressed over the impact that such a difficult season had on people like Burns and Michels, who he thought very highly of as friends and mentors.

In some respects, Steckel might have been a man ahead of his time while coaching in the NFL. Steckel reacted similarly to coaches today in a few ways, while other attempts were not even close. So it didn't work out, and his legacy will remain tainted in the eyes of the faithful forever.

But Les Steckel is a good man and an honest man who looks back with sensitivity and care on those who were hurt and discouraged by his wares during his only year in charge of the Purple.

One of Steckel's proudest moments as a coach came in a game familiar to most loyal, long-term Viking fans. The famous Kramer to Rashad Hail Mary pass in the closing moments of the Cleveland game that sent Minnesota to the playoffs in 1980 will go down as one of the greatest moments in Vikings history. However, few recall the play before Kramer's last-second pass. Tommy Kramer threw over the middle to Joe Senser, who immediately pitched the ball out to Ted Brown. The running back relentlessly ran up the sidelines, putting the Vikings in position for the last-minute miracle.

The Steckel-designed play was met with success partially because of Ted Brown, who had the intelligence to quickly step out of bounds as he went up the field. Had Brown not done this, time would have elapsed and the game would have been over, one play short of victory.

The Vikings started the drive deep in their own territory. They knew they had time for only two plays. Grant looked to Jerry Burns and asked, "Whaddya got?" Steckel recalls Burns' reply: "We got that ##%#$%# play of Steckel's!" Grant said back to Burns, "Seriously, Jerry, whaddya got?" Burns again replied, "We got that ##%#$%# play of Steckel's!" Well, Steckel's ##%#$%# play worked and put the Vikings into position for the famous heroics of Tommy Kramer and Ahmad Rashad.

Steckel was fired after the 1984 season, and Bud returned for one more year in 1985. Steckel says he is the answer to one of the most famous NFL trivia questions of all time. The question is, "Who was the Vikings' head coach between Bud Grant and Bud Grant?"

"Busy" is an understatement when describing the life of Les Steckel today. He is the national president of the Fellowship of Christian Athletes and travels and speaks extensively. Another head coaching job is perhaps looming out there on the horizon. After all, coaching at 37 years of age is quite different than coaching some two decades later. We all wish we knew as much the day we started a job as the day we left it.

When Grant left once more, the great offensive genius of the Vikings, Jerry Burns, became the man in charge. Burns' reputation as a strategist and great football mind was unquestioned and he had some outstanding years, coming just one play away from a Super Bowl during one season as head coach.

"Burnsie," as he is called by the many who love him, did a great job throughout the six years he ran the Vikings.

"He treated me so well," says Les Steckel. "I never worked for anyone better than Jerry Burns."

"Jerry Burns is a character," says Mike Lynn. "He is a different breed, a very likeable guy. I don't think you could find a person who has had a run-in with him."

"He has the smartest football mind I have ever known," says longtime Vikings employee Paul Wiggin. This is quite a statement of significance coming from a person who has been involved in professional and college football for over 50 years.

Bob Sansevere, sports reporter for the *St. Paul Pioneer Press*, says, "Jerry Burns is the most underrated head coach Minnesota ever had."

Sansevere truly enjoyed covering the Vikings when Burns was the head coach. "I knew I could always hit his hot buttons if I asked him a question in one of three areas," says Sansevere. "If I asked him about a quarterback controversy, the Herschel Walker trade, or if the Vikings had the killer instinct, I knew I had hit the hot button!" The reporter shows a great deal of respect for Burns.

Because the head coach had an incredible hatred for and fear of most insects and other unusual species, Burns was susceptible to many a beloved prank. Spiders crawling across the ceiling, a furry creature residing in the coach's desk drawers, or a fake snake flying out of a movie projector were all fair game when showing affection for one of the most beloved Vikings of all time. Regardless, Jerry Burns was a great football coach and a winner both on and off the field, which he demonstrated with the team for 24 seasons.

---

Offensive mastermind Jerry Burns remained the Vikings' head coach from 1986 to 1991. *Photo courtesy of the Minnesota Vikings*

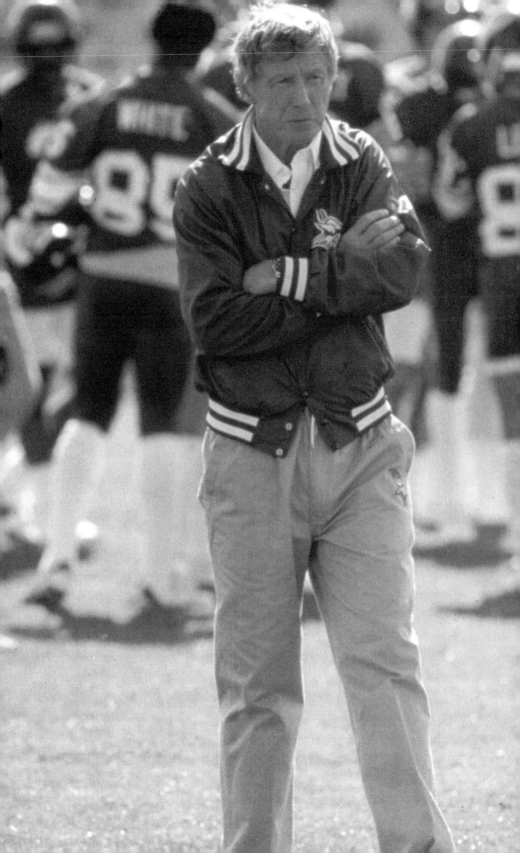

In 1992, Roger Headrick became president and chief operating officer of the Minnesota Vikings. He was a solid and experienced businessman, and went about his first major task in a professional and businesslike manner. His first major decision, the hiring of Dennis Green as the team's next head coach, was a success.

During the decade-plus years that Green coached the Vikings, they won and they won often. His high-flying, vertical offense threw the ball frequently and repeatedly long down the field. Being blessed with great players like Randy Moss, Cris Carter, Randall Cunningham, and Daunte Culpepper didn't hurt either.

Pete Bercich, drafted by the Minnesota Vikings in 1995 out of the University of Notre Dame, played for the Vikings for seven years and coached four more. "Dennis Green put a lot of emphasis on who you were as an individual and where you came from, as opposed to what kind of player you were," says Bercich. "He saw something in people, and he told us to 'know our role and accept it.' He always treated us well and had a plan and stuck with it."

Green won many games and was a regular in the playoffs; however, he got little recognition for his deep commitment to the community. The coach felt strongly that the Vikings needed to interact and give back to the area and insisted on it from his players as well as himself. "Community Tuesdays" and their true significance can be traced to Dennis Green and his strong belief that the Vikings needed to be out in the community on a regular basis.

Fred Zamberletti, longtime Viking legend, speaks of Green in high regard. "He never got the credit that he deserved for his community work," says Zamberletti. "He wanted the players to be good citizens and it hurt him deeply when someone did something to hurt what he believed in."

Zamberletti recalls how Green supported the concept of voting in the intercity. His effort in that regard recorded some of the highest voting numbers due directly to work in the area. Green visited nursing homes, brought kids from Chicago who made good grades

Former head coach Dennis Green maintained a strong winning record while with the Minnesota Vikings. *Photo courtesy of the Minnesota Vikings*

in school to Viking games, and was involved in grade school reading programs. He provided never-ending support for community work with little need for recognition.

Bob Hagan, Vikings Director of Public Relations, speaks of Green's connection to the area. "Denny was very community-driven," recalls Hagan. "He expected the players to be out in the community on Tuesdays. The players always knew Denny was serious about his expectations. They always knew he was in charge. He was also very focused about football."

Viking Pro Bowl center Matt Birk speaks highly of Green with devout loyalty. "I had instant respect for him from the first time I saw him," says Birk. "When I would see him in the hall, it was like seeing the principal. He and Mike Tice brought me in here to the Vikings and gave me a chance. I will never forget what they did for me as a player and a person. They told me that I was their guy and that they believed in me. For those guys to have that kind of faith in me, it meant a lot."

Paul Wiggin first met Dennis Green many years back when they were together at Stanford University. Their relationship has spanned decades. "He is an outstanding football coach and an outstanding motivator of players," recalls Wiggin.

"I liked him very much," says Fred Zamberletti. "He always treated me with dignity and respect. He was a good husband and father and a good football coach. Sometimes, it seemed as if he held things together with bailing wire. He arrived as Viking coach with few top draft choices due to the Walker trade and lost a lot of players due to financial constraints, yet he never complained."

Toward the end of the 2001 season, Dennis Green left the Vikings. Mike Tice was made interim coach and stayed four more seasons as the head coach of the Minnesota Vikings.

Tice was a likeable sort and came with a strong resume. He was a player and a fine offensive line coach for over a decade in the NFL. He treated players and people in general very well, and had an open and, for the most part, decent relationship with the media. In addition, he was a good football coach with a credible win-loss record.

In some respects, Tice held things together by a shoestring. The money for free agent players and new contracts was stressed under Red McCombs, and the then-owner underspent on assistant coaches as well; however, Tice fared pretty well overall.

He was well liked by most of the players and staff that worked around him. A tough head coach in most respects, he demanded a great deal from his coaches and players.

"I thought he was a fun guy to work for," says Paul Wiggin. "We always had a great working relationship. Mike was very glib and also very clever. Sometimes his openness gave away too much information. In addition, he was a great offensive line coach!"

"He was one of my favorite coaches," says Bob Sansevere. Mike was always very open with the media, and for a sports reporter like Bob, it made the job very appealing.

Pete Bercich was the linebackers' coach under Tice. "I thought he was very unique and very passionate," says Bercich. "You always knew where you stood with Mike. He was very detailed and a well-organized person. And he was a very demanding coach."

Matt Birk also holds Mike Tice in very high regard. "He was a former player," says Birk. "He really understands what a player goes through. He was a college quarterback who really had to work hard to make the team, and we related well to that."

Birk further described Tice, saying, "He was tough to play for, and he excelled at making you mentally tough." Little question remains that the "tough to play for" as described by Birk was given in an appreciative and accepting manner, pointing out Tice's strengths as a dedicated and commanding coach.

Tice was very family centered and wanted his players to focus on family as well. "He used to tell us to 'call home,'" says Birk, "and was always thinking of the importance of players keeping in touch with their families."

Tice took great pride in his position as the leader of the Purple. Following his fourth year as head coach of the team, the Vikings' new ownership determined it was time for a new direction, and Mike Tice was fired after the final game of the 2005 season. His tenure as a player, offensive line coach, and head coach of the Minnesota Vikings was over.

The Wilf ownership group named Brad Childress to lead the Purple. Childress, a longtime respected assistant in the Philadelphia Eagles' organization, took over early in 2006 for the Vikings' 46th season.

Reporter Bob Sansevere has formed an early opinion of the head coach, as they are in the early stages of their relationship. "I like the guy," says Sansevere. "He has a sense of humor and is easy to talk to one on one."

Legendary pro football great Paul Wiggin speaks highly of Brad Childress' character. "He believes in the right things," says Paul. It's the kind of complement that is crucial to setting the right type of standards for an organization. Childress has made many of the right moves thus far surrounding his high expectations for behavior off the field of play."

Although far too early to judge the new head coach, it has been early determined that Childress is a strict disciplinarian and devoted to a system of controlling the football.

"A football team has to be disciplined," says Childress. "We are getting there." He is very strong in his convictions in this regard, and believes his football team is on the right track. He wants to win and he wants to win badly, but only with the right kind of people. As the new leader of the beloved Purple, this is extremely important to Brad Childress.

He has separated his coaching style from that of Tice, Green, Burns, Steckel, Grant, and Van Brocklin—and that he should. To be successful in the NFL, one must be his own individual, as were the others before him.

Childress greatly appreciates being only one of 32 to hold the title of head coach in the NFL. But there is more to it than just that. He truly recognizes the meaning of being the Minnesota Vikings head coach. "There are great people in this area. They have great passion for the Vikings," says Childress.

In February of 2007, the coach spoke before Roundy's Club in Red Wing, Minnesota. The club's founder, Noel Evans, named the club some 44 years ago after sports reporter Roundy Coughlin, who once headlined the local program "Roundy Predicts" decades ago.

"Coach Childress gave a great personal speech," says Noel Evans. "It came straight from the heart. And when it was over, many people raced to the front of the room to shake hands with the coach. He stayed for an hour after, talking with and greeting those in attendance." He made Noel Evans very proud.

After their close interaction with the new coach, many of the club members came away from the event with a positive impression, one much different than what is often portrayed in the media and seen on television or from the stands in the heat of the game on Sunday afternoons. True character, what is in the heart and soul of an individual, isn't always made public near the goal posts or between the chalk lines.

Brad Childress is a good football coach who plans to carry on a winning tradition. And as the faithful wait, he will, as he so often has stated, determine his own fate. "We are judged by the number of games we win," says Childress. No one would expect it to be any different for him.

# 10

# THE WILFS'
# OWNERSHIP

THEY WERE NEW YORK GIANTS FANS! Competing in the Meadowlands, players like Frank Gifford, Charlie Connerly, and the great Sam Huff made up a part of the fabulous franchise of the east. The media once made a film called *The Violent World of Sam Huff*, glamorizing the ferocious middle linebacker and his pack of legendary football men of mortal fame and glory.

They cheered for the romanticism of the NFL, football in the "Big Apple," and for the Giants' name to stand alone as a symbol of the immortal men who adorned the name of the team's great city on the side of their royal blue headgear.

It was New York Giants football and fame, and they loved it with a passion and deep respect. They cheered when the New York Giants won and roared when they beat the Minnesota Vikings in the NFC Championship game at the Meadowlands on January 14, 2001.

The score was 41-0. Minnesota fans bled and toiled in the great loss, while they flourished in the win. They were Giants fans through and through.

But their passion for the game has changed colors ... AND THEY NOW OWN THE MINNESOTA VIKINGS!

On May 25, 2005, NFL owners unanimously approved new ownership for the beloved Purple. An investment group, led by brothers Zygmunt and Mark Wilf, took full control of the Vikings

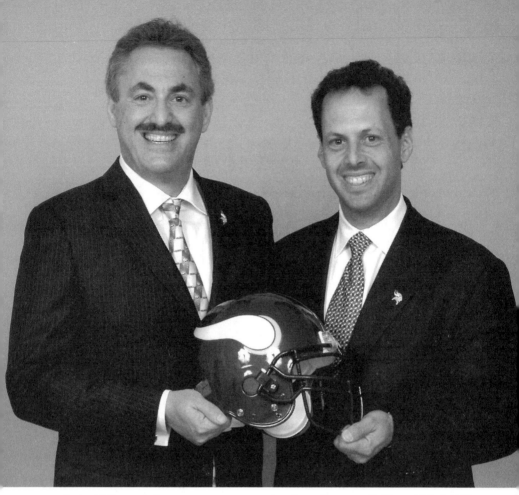

Part of Minnesota's new owners group, brothers Zygmunt (left) and Mark Wilf have become leaders in the franchise. *Photo courtesy of the Minnesota Vikings*

organization from the previous owner, Red McCombs, in mid-June of 2005. McCombs had owned the Vikings since 1998.

The Wilf family, owners of a real estate development company in New Jersey, are joined in ownership by cousin Leonard Wilf and nephew Jeffrey Wilf, along with Reggie Fowler, David Mandelbaum, and Alan Landis.

Throughout the initial stages of its development, the new leadership group's record of commitment to the franchise and the beginning of a love for the Men who wear the Purple has been evident. During their first year as owners, they have accomplished one of the most productive off-seasons in team history.

Signing Brad Childress as the new head coach of the Vikings was not the only major step taken. The organization has begun the process of providing the Purple with the necessary ingredients, enhancing the roster by signing high-priced, quality free agents.

The Wilfs' commitment as new owners to the organization showed early as they made impressive changes to the Winter Park headquarters and training facility. Improvements to the locker room, athletic training area, and equipment facilities have been dramatic and greatly appreciated within the organization.

Initiated into the limelight of the NFL, the Wilfs have also been relatively well received by one of the Vikings' local sports reporters. Judd Zulgad writes for the *Minneapolis Star Tribune*, and has been impressed thus far with the team's new ownership.

"The Wilfs love football and they want to do what is right," says Judd. "The family has a good moral compass." Coming from a reporter around Vikings headquarters most every day, this is quite an endorsement for what lies ahead in the land where all wear purple.

Zygmunt, or Zygi Wilf, the principal owner and frontal face of the franchise, has been active in communicating to the staff, the fans, and the region that the Minnesota Vikings are about winning, respect, honor, and integrity. He has made it publicly well known that the team will flourish with top-quality, skillful individuals recognized by their credibility and integrity.

The Wilfs profess their passion with little hesitation over one of their favorite expressions, "Doing what's right." They make the comment with sincere meaning and deeply believe in operating their business and personal lives in this regard.

"It was a lifetime dream of ours to own an NFL franchise," says a proud Mark Wilf, president of the Minnesota Vikings. "We love football, and we knew of the great history of the Vikings and have great admiration for the history of the sport," says Mark. "And remember, we had Fran Tarkenton with the Giants before he returned to the Vikings."

So a connection did exist between the Wilfs and the Vikings, even when they were Giants fans. And in the mind of principal owner Zygi Wilf, the Vikings, an NFC team with a long winning history, had captured his passion for many years before he became the owner. "We could not have had a better situation than the Vikings," says Zygi. His goal of owning an NFL franchise was apparently just meant to be.

The Wilf family's ultimate desire is to build a winning organization with the right type of people. They cannot emphasize enough how "doing the right thing" becomes the foundational premise with everything they have set out to accomplish.

"I think we are on the right track," says Mark Wilf. "We are trying to get the right kind of people put into place to win a championship with the right character. We are very confident in what we are doing, and we believe Brad Childress is the right person for the job. He knows football, is a straight shooter, and he is a person of character. We are building a chemistry within our organization to win—but win by doing it the right way."

"When we selected Brad Childress to be the head coach, we knew it was a step in the right direction," says Zygi Wilf. Childress unquestionably fills the mold created by the Wilfs and represents what they want in a head coach.

With this philosophy intact and a history of success, little doubt remains that the Wilfs are committed, hard-working people. "We are going to put together a team to win the championship," says Zygi Wilf. "But we are going to do it with the right people and the right way. We are committed to run the Minnesota Vikings like we have run our family business," says Zygi. "We have become successful with the right character of people."

When the Wilfs speak of winning, bringing about a successful NFL franchise, accomplishing the goal of a Super Bowl championship, or with respect to any other aspect of their Vikings operation, one can rest assured that the commentary will end something to the effect of "with the right people," "with the right character," "by doing it the right way," or "by doing the right thing." It is what they believe and, with the highest form of passion and dignity, they are not afraid to express it.

When listening to the Wilfs' intensity over their beliefs, it is obvious that their passion does not come from their lips, but rather from their hearts and their souls. They are good people who truly want to do what's right with the right kind of people and character. They won't have it any other way.

Mark Wilf brings his ideals, integrity, and forthrightness right to the heart of the issue. "We want the fans to know this organization is working hard every minute of every day to bring a championship to Minnesota for all the great Viking fans ... but with the right kind of people." He cannot make the ownership's goals clearer.

Hiring Brad Childress was a signature example of the type of leadership and quality of character expected for the franchise in the future. Early on in his role as the new head coach, Childress proved his commitment to fielding quality personnel by "sending a strong message" to the players, fans, and the organization, making difficult decisions due to off-the-field misconduct.

Coach Childress is all business, powerfully committed to having quality personnel represent the Minnesota Vikings football team. "I want guys in this building who treat the janitor or the people in payroll the same as they treat me," says Childress. "We want good players who are good people."

Childress speaks with great passion and pride over the community commitment of players like Matt Birk, Steve Hutchinson, and Tony Richardson. "They give what they have to the less fortunate," says the coach. To Childress, these players represent the Vikings as "good players and good people."

Spending time with Brad Childress quickly proves that the Wilfs knew exactly what they were doing when they made the commitment to turn the Men of Purple over to his charge. They are owners to whom "family" is important and dignity and honor are givens. Childress' internal beliefs lie within the same values, and he practices them daily.

The head coach understands the importance of winning as well. He knows the number of victories and defeats will ultimately judge him. But there is little doubt that the wins will come about by, as Childress often says, "doing the right thing." He preaches this to his players and mentions it to others. "It is about trust. Do the right thing," is Brad Childress' foundational premise, providing the cornerstone for all that is proper and correct in his system of values. And it cannot and will not be compromised.

The owners and the coach sing from the same hymnal, and that sets the tone for a good beginning. During the Vikings' interview process for the head coaching position, Childress learned a great deal about the new owners, perhaps as much as they learned about him. He saw their passion and incredible desire to win on Sundays in the fall. But more importantly, he saw something else.

Brad Childress saw "family people with strong family values," and knew he wanted to work for them. "They sold themselves to me as to who they were," says Childress.

So the Vikings and the new owners got themselves a football coach. Along with a solid background in coaching, Childress brings the following principles:

"Do the right thing."

"Be good players who are good people."

"You cannot be seduced by just good athletic ability."

"Treat the janitor the same as you treat me."

"Give what you have to the less fortunate."

"Give back to the community on days off."

"Treat people the way you want to be treated."

"Football is the ultimate team game, and we want a 'we' mentality, not 'I'."

This is what Brad Childress is all about. A passion for winning and the pride and satisfaction that go with it are unquestionably always present within the head coach. But his enthusiasm for giving back is just as strong and becomes evident when he says, "You see the eyes on the kids." What it means to his heart when the Vikings have made a difference in a youngster's life is easy to read; you can see it in the eyes of the coach when he mentions "giving back."

A long list of excellent credentials, a passion to win, and the satisfaction of giving back to others, along with a love of the game, come with the Childress package. Kevin Costner starred in a movie

Along with the Wilfs, current head coach Brad Childress has big plans for the Vikings. *Photo courtesy of the Minnesota Vikings*

a few years back entitled *For Love of the Game*. The film was about a longtime successful pitcher by the name of Billy Chappell, who pitched in the big leagues for 19 seasons for the Detroit Tigers and did it in a manner full of such passion and pride it could only be *For Love of the Game*.

The theme of that movie is inside the heart and soul of the new Minnesota Vikings coach, except his infatuation and appreciation are for an oval ball rather than a round one.

"I want players who love the game," says the Viking leader. "I want them to be the kind of people who enjoy everything about it—the practices, the conditioning, the pressures, the anguish, all parts of it."

The coach uses the example of Vikings first rounder in the 2006 draft, Chad Greenway. "He loves the game. He is out fielding punts before practice," says Childress. "You can tell the guys who love the game."

Childress' thinking also coincides with what longtime Viking Scott Studwell strongly believes in. "I'm excited about what Brad is doing," says Studwell, looking toward a bright and positive future for Vikings football. "And I also know the organization is led by people who truly want to do the right thing. They want to win and do it the right way. They want employees who want to come to work. They are very genuine people who listen to what others have to say. They care about people and are not driven by financial factors."

The Wilfs' passion for football, family values, and belief in doing what is right, combined with Brad Childress' commitment to winning, credibility, love for the game, and desire to give back, may be meant to be. Only the future will tell and, at this time, only the future knows for sure. But with the team's development in the most positive of directions, the odds are in favor of it all.

In addition to honoring an early commitment to improve their team on the field, the Wilfs have demonstrated their plan to better connect the Vikings to their surroundings. They have increased the community relations budget and have diligently supported and endorsed both the players' and organization's ties to the community.

Lester Bagley, vice president of public affairs/stadium development, has been directly involved in the Vikings' stadium efforts for several years. He speaks proudly of the organization's plan for redevelopment in downtown Minneapolis and the Wilfs' long-term commitment to the new stadium plan.

Some of us were there for the Vikings' beginning at the old Metropolitan Stadium in Bloomington, and some of us were there for the opening game at the Metrodome, cheering on our beloved Purple.

Now some of us begin to revel in the thought of a new home for the Purple to roam, with the chance to breathe in fresh air on beautiful Sundays in the fall. The newness and importance of a dwelling deserving of the warriors and the faithful who have cherished them are on the horizon.

With the Wilfs, belief and hope exist, and a brightness glows in the reality of the future for the team, the fans, and the region.

"The Wilf family is in it for the long haul," says Lester. "They have established their commitment and credibility through their willingness to put hundreds of millions of dollars into the economy through economic development.

"We are very fortunate the Wilf family are the owners of the Minnesota Vikings. They have provided a 'refreshing' operation and have made a strong commitment to the community," says Bagley. "'Giving back' is a strong belief of the Wilfs'." The words are part of their vocabulary with the definition in the results, which have proven worthy of the very highest of esteem.

The new Vikings owners are not inexperienced when it comes to operating a successful business organization. The group's past history has recorded national recognition for their skills in business ventures with Garden Homes Development, prominently at the forefront in leadership of retail and private residential development.

Commitment to philanthropic causes and the desire to honor the history of their family has been instrumental as the driving force behind the Wilfs' successful and honorable ventures.

A word often referenced by the Wilfs and Brad Childress when speaking of the future of the Minnesota Vikings, "family" has led to the successes of the past and will surely lead to the successes in years to come.

And it starts at the top with a commitment and desire to "do the right thing." The Wilfs' family history and deeply centered value system is now in charge at Winter Park, home of the beloved Purple.

A new pride exists in the Northland, and those in control have traded in their royal blue headgear for a helmet of purple with horns above the ears.

# 11

# PURPLE
# REVIEW

"ANTICIPATION AND APPRECIATION" are the words often used by former legendary Vikings coach Bud Grant when describing the significance of living in the Northland.

He speaks of the frigid conditions of winter and how much we "anticipate" the arrival of spring. And when these climate modifications occur with the appearance of flowers, beautiful sunshine, and warmer weather, we "appreciate" and enjoy the new and fresh change in seasons.

Through the progression of summer and the heat and humidity of July and August, we "anticipate" fall's glory and the cool evenings aside the magnificent, color-changing leaves. Another season of "appreciation" is cast upon us.

Grant makes it all so easy. He just has a way of putting things in the proper order and perspective. And while he's always kept life in the simplest of ways, he was also the football coach of the Minnesota Vikings for 18 seasons.

He was the man in charge for almost two decades. He truly understood the game, his coaches and players, and so much more about life. Grant is a "naturalist" and knows how to enjoy life outside the competitive arena of professional football.

Former Vikings running back Jim Lindsey says that Grant would perhaps be content to travel deep into the woods only to lie in the snow and watch a family of deer all day. Outside his commitment to family and friends, all Grant really expected from life was to enjoy the outdoors, accompanied by a rifle or fishing rod.

The former head coach has raised ducks, geese, skunks, birds, and an occasional raven, certainly making life interesting. On occasion, guests at his cabin have watched in amazement as ducks, geese, and other birds respond to his whistle, fly in, and gather around him— much like the Men of Purple once did every fall Sunday.

Nurturing animals through understanding compassion isn't much different from supporting men in the violent world of professional football. He was the Vikings' leader, they counted and depended on him, and he rarely let them down.

Bud Grant is quick to express his deep regard and appreciation for the many staff members and coaches who, by excelling in their jobs, made him successful. He has always been able to see the larger picture in life, and gives recognition where it is due.

Longtime former Vikings employee Kernal Buhler has an interesting way of describing the former field leader. "Bud Grant is an area icon," says Kernal. "He is a person that someone working in marketing dreams about. He is tough, a winner, respected, oblivious to the cold weather of Minnesota, and a great athlete from here. It was such a great fit."

When asked for the list of mentors and inspirational contacts throughout his successful life and legendary career, Grant speaks of only one person ultimately responsible for who he is today. He gives his wife of 57 years, Pat, all credit and appreciation.

His face becomes radiant and his eyes gleam when he speaks of his beloved Pat. She knows and understands him, and it is abundantly clear how greatly he recognizes the meaning she brings to his life. "She is my greatest attribute," says a proud Bud Grant.

Most people would profess that their positive learning experiences have come from watching the successes of others, but Grant has a unique approach. He developed and learned football fame from studying the negative and making sure he did things in an approach different from observed failures.

"I watched and learned from what didn't work, and used my knowledge and experience to make decisions that had chances for success," says Grant. "Don't make a decision unless you have to. Some might call it procrastinating." But in his way of thinking, "the best decision might just become more clear in the morning."

Emotion runs deep in the heart of Bud Grant when he talks about his former players. He is quick to point out the wonderful athletic abilities of those who adorned the purple colors beside him and the special qualities of the many who he judged in the fall.

Like his life, his coaching technique was simple. He appreciated the personalities and cherished the bond he shared with his players. Although Bud Grant never speaks of a favorite, he does talk about one Viking with special affection. He wore No. 70. His name was Jim Marshall, and he was something special.

"Jim bought the program. His longevity was amazing. He started and played every game. I owe a great debt to Jim Marshall. He never bent, bled, or broke," recalls Grant. "I can remember when Jim twisted his ankle so badly that we were sure he would be out of action for six weeks. He started the next game.

"Of all the players through the years, he epitomizes the Minnesota Vikings," says Bud Grant. "I love Jim Marshall!"

The man the faithful know best as "Bud" left the field where the Purple play some 20 years ago, but remains a legendary part of Vikings lore "due to the graciousness of the franchise leadership," says Grant. He still has an office in Winter Park and uses it most days. Whether through answering letters, taking phone calls, or reminiscing about football, the Vikings remain a part of his life. And he remains a part of the Vikings.

About a half-dozen letters and sometimes as many as 15 to 20 phone calls a day keep Grant pretty busy. The faithful remember what he did for the Vikings and the region, and he still speaks of the pride and honor he feels to have been a part of it all.

Perhaps Paul Wiggin, who has spent 50 years around college and professional football, sums it up best: "If you are lucky enough to have Bud Grant come into your office and sit down for a chat, you will have experienced enough from the conversation similar to having completed a five-credit course."

Great Purple memories certainly deserving of a spot in Vikings lore rest with the purple jersey Nos. 58, 59, and 60. These numbers and the players who wore them, alongside each other for many seasons, are symbolic of the great passion, pride, and union these three individuals brought to the team.

Faithful Vikings fans often recall the many great players who wore the Purple and sported the helmets with the horns on the side. One of those who patrolled the right outside linebacker position for 12 years from 1968 to 1979 was No. 58, Wally Hilgenberg.

Hilgenberg, a superb athlete out of the University of Iowa released by the Pittsburgh Steelers and picked up by Minnesota, joined forces with No. 59, Lonnie Warwick, and No. 60, Roy Winston, to make up the Vikings' linebacker corps for many years.

A special friendship formed within this group of tough, hard-nosed players, remaining intact some 40 years later. Not only has the group remained good friends, but the bond among them has remarkable appeal.

Wally Hilgenberg's initials, W.W.H, stand for Walter William Hilgenberg. Roy Winston played left side linebacker and Lonnie Warwick played middle linebacker. So the first "W" in Hilgenberg's initials signified Winston on the left, the second "W" represented Warwick in the middle, and the "H" stood for Hilgenberg on the right. It gets better, however.

When Hilgenberg was 58 years old, his age and old Vikings' number matched. At the same time, Warwick was 59 years old and Winston was 60; both their numbers equaled their ages as well. Unusual? Well, there is more.

When Wally Hilgenberg joined the Vikings in 1968, he asked Warwick and Winston if he could go hunting with them. The first time he joined them to go duck hunting was the beginning of a longtime hunting relationship among the three. Winston drove that initial morning, picking the others up in his green Chevy pickup truck.

As their companionship grew and the hunting trips became more regular, the three noticed their trips had a routine similarity.

Winston was always the driver, Warwick sat in the middle, and Hilgenberg took the outside right.

From left to right: 60, 59, and 58; Winston, Warwick, and Hilgenberg. From right to left: 58, 59 and 60; Hilgenberg, Warwick, and Winston. The arrangement was always the same.

The bond among these three former Vikings was symbolic of the football team's connections to one another at the time. Looking at the Vikings' defense from the rear, Winston, No. 60, played left outside linebacker, Warwick, No. 59, was at middle linebacker, and Hilgenberg, No. 58, performed as right outside linebacker. The ironies all made sense and likely existed for a reason, symbolizing their great friendship as significant members of the Minnesota Vikings.

The three were friends on and off the field and were always accountable to one another. On their first hunting trip together, Winston and Warwick advised Hilgenberg to bring a pair of waders. He went out and bought a new pair and started to put them on early in the morning as the three arrived near a river to hunt ducks.

As he dressed, Hilgenberg noticed that Winston and Warwick weren't putting on their waders. When he asked them about it, he was told they didn't have any. It took only seconds for him to realize the waders were his initiation into the friendship, as he would be the one going into the river to put out the decoys that morning.

"Waders? We don't have any waders!" Hilgenberg just needed a pair to belong. For Nos. 58, 59, and 60, it has been a wonderful friendship lasting close to four decades.

Through the years, such connections have made the Minnesota Vikings special. Dan Endy worked for the organization in the front office from 1982 to 1993 and has many reflections on this subject.

He recalls Larry "Stosh" Nueman, former Vikings assistant trainer under Fred Zamberletti. "Stosh developed cancer and became very ill. Former general manager Mike Lynn had told him as long as he could walk through the front door, he would have a job with the Vikings," says Endy.

Near the end of his life, Stosh could barely tape a player's ankle. Endy and longtime Vikings equipment manager, Dennis Ryan, recall how Pat Eilers, former Viking, always had Stosh tape his ankles before every practice. He would then have to remove the tape and have someone else redo the job in another area. It was the Viking way.

Endy was involved in public relations and operations and became close with many of the great Vikings players. In his opinion, "no player better understood his role with the media than Tommy Kramer." Endy loved working with the athlete. "He had such a professional toughness and moxie about him," says Endy.

Dan Endy also had a special fondness for former coach Jerry Burns. He always sat next to Burns on the bus when the Vikings traveled to out-of-town games. "He could recite the entire game in his head afterward," says Endy. "Trust me, he always knew what was going on."

The memories go on and on for Dan Endy, and he speaks of them with great sentiment. "My all-time favorite player would have to be Scott Studwell," Endy says. "He was a genuine person and such a hard worker. He made the Pro Bowls and he paid attention to the little things. He truly played for the love of the game."

Studwell played from 1977 to 1990, and left every ounce of his athletic ability on the field every single game. He was a magnificent player and, as the team's director of college scouting, has kept his connection with the Vikings intact.

It might be very difficult to find someone who loves his job more than Scott Studwell. He beams when speaking of the opportunities he has had in professional football. "I thank my lucky stars every day for what I have been able to do. It is a 'labor of love' for me," says Studwell. He played 14 years in the NFL and has been on the Vikings' management team for the past 16 years.

Loyalty is a word that rests at the top of Studwell's vocabulary. "Even with free agency as it is today, I would have, as a player, taken less money to stay with the Minnesota Vikings," he says. "I know how very fortunate I am to be here, and I owe a lot to the Viking organization."

Studwell was drafted in the ninth round out of the University of Illinois. A ninth-round draft choice playing for 14 years is almost unbelievable. Obviously, all the intricacies that went into evaluating talent had no method for measuring the size of Scott Studwell's heart.

According to the *Viking Media Guide*, in his years with the Vikings, Studwell recorded more tackles than any one player with the same organization in the history of the NFL. And you don't achieve that record with only athletic ability!

He loves the game and played hard every second. He speaks with an exuberance of pride over his good fortune of having joined the Vikings when illustrious players of the past were still around. "I came in when the greats were still here. Players like Jim Marshall, Tarkenton, Tingelhoff, Eller, and Bill Brown. They knew how to win, and they always found ways to win," says Studwell. "They were here forever and they played because they loved the game."

Studwell also speaks to the leadership of Bud Grant during those glory years and how he handled the team. "Bud Grant has the most common-sense approach to the game of anyone I have ever been around," Studwell says. "He never missed a trick. He always knew what to do."

Studwell's approach to his work in the front office is the same as when he put on the uniform. Although hitting people is not appropriate these days, devotion to his responsibilities doesn't take a back seat to any other part of his career. "We are striving every day for a reputation as a hardworking organization," says Studwell. "The Minnesota Vikings are a staple to the community and we are a bunch of people trying our very best to bring a championship to Minnesota."

"I tell young players today they need to recognize it is a privilege to do what they do and they must look at it that way. They need to understand that football is fun," Studwell continues. "We try to find players with good character and who love the game."

If one could mold a player whose mind-set worked in coordination with his athletic ability and whose passion lasted beyond a playing career into his next endeavor, the name Scott Studwell would be inscribed on the cast. It might even read something like, "Wouldn't it be a wonderful game if everyone played and gave with the passion and love of Scott Studwell?" This praise sounds similar to the monumental tribute once paid to the great Hugh McElhenny years back.

This year signifies Studwell's third full decade with the Vikings. Knowing the former athlete is still around has given the organization comfort the last 30 years.

Other former Vikings players also had a great love for the game. One of those wore No. 41 from 1965 to 1975, coming to the Vikings from the University of North Dakota. His name was Dave Osborn. He was a tough, hard-nosed running back who knew how to play the game one way: with every ounce of energy he had in him.

"I was just happy to be here. I would have played for only room and board," says Osborn. "I loved to play the game. I am so proud of who I played with. I played with Hall of Famers and I played with a group of guys who were great players. They still remain my best friends."

"We played with the Vikings for a long time together. It was a team game and we played for each other," Osborn explains. "We had desire, pride, a competitive spirit, and we played with pain. These were hardworking, honest, intelligent players who were also good friends."

They believed they could win, and they were right. And they did it on a routine basis for many years.

The team concept played itself out in 1974, when the Vikings finished the regular season at Kansas City. Osborn needed to run for 28 yards in the game to achieve a sizeable bonus for total yards gained during the season.

Before the game, Bud Grant came to Osborn and Bill Brown and told them they were going to be rested for the game so they would be ready for the playoffs. The Vikings had clinched a playoff berth and saw little need to risk either injuries or fatigue going into the postseason.

Osborn recalls thinking at the time, "'There goes my bonus.' But I was not about to say anything. This was not about me. It was about the team. That's just the way it was."

But it worked out anyway. Osborn was on the kickoff special teams. On the opening play of the game, the Kansas City kicker squib kicked the ball down the field. It bounced right to Osborn, who returned the ball up the field for 30 yards. A coincidence? Maybe. A true Purple moment? Most assuredly!

Another memorable moment for Dave Osborn shows the affection the Vikings' players had for each other in those glory years of the past. Many of them had played together for over a decade. They were close as players and closer as friends.

In 1976, Dave Osborn was released at the end of training camp. He had pondered retirement and accepted his release. Several weeks into the season, his first as a non-player since 1965, Osborn received a call from Bart Starr, coach of the rival Green Bay Packers. The result led him to finishing his last year in pro football wearing green and gold.

Under Bud Grant, the Vikings always arrived at the stadium one hour before game time, which allowed little time for dressing, pregame warm-ups, etc. It was Grant's way. The Packers, on the other hand, arrived several hours before game time.

This particular week, the Packers were playing the Vikings at the old Metropolitan Stadium in Bloomington, Minnesota. Osborn arrived early with the Packers and went directly to the Vikings' vacant locker room. He proceeded to tie many of the players' jerseys and other apparel into tight knots, making shambles of their dress garb. It allowed the Vikings little time to get their gear in order before the game. Osborn had made a mess of things for his former colleagues.

Metropolitan Stadium was the only field at the time that had both home and visiting benches on the same side of the field. This made it easy for Osborn to hear chants from the Vikings' sideline throughout most of the game. "We'll get you for that, Osborn!" they howled. "You have no place to hide. You are going to get yours, Osborn, just you wait!"

Once the game ended, Osborn immediately took off running for the tunnel at the opposite side of the field; however, several Vikings had the angle and caught him before he escaped to safety. It was a sad sight to see as the Purple lot stuffed the green and gold traitor in a large snow bank in the adjacent end zone.

But snow in his face, on his helmet and uniform was a small price to pay for the dishonor and trouble he afforded his pals and their uniforms. In retrospect, maybe they were just some big kids playing in the snow with their friend, remembering the time they all wore the Purple.

As Minnesota's equipment manager, Dennis Ryan has been handling Vikings equipment since 1975. He loves his job and is proud to speak about his role with the Vikings. "My kids' friends' dads have all kinds of different jobs in different professions, and no one is really sure what they actually do every day. But all my kids' friends know what I do as the Vikings' equipment manager," says Ryan.

Ryan started helping the Vikings move equipment to training camp in the mid-'70s. He worked the ground crew at Midway Stadium in St. Paul and made a connection with the Vikings when they used the stadium as their practice facility.

Ryan speaks of the great Vikings tradition and the superstitions that go with it relating to equipment. Certain players always want certain things certain ways. "Jim Marshall always had to have the same shoelaces no matter what the condition," smiles Ryan. It apparently didn't matter if they were ragged, tied in knots, and barely keeping the shoes on—they could not be changed.

The Vikings were very special, and Ryan recalls how the NFL followed in the Vikings' footsteps through the years as they transformed the ways things were done. Often, the Vikings' uniform dress was symbolic of the league's wishes. "The NFL took Bud Grant's approach to how the uniform should be worn," says Ryan. The Vikings' way was successful and set an example for the rest of the teams to follow.

As a longtime Vikings employee, Dennis Ryan has been a part of many interesting moments. Such times include one rainy night in Oakland when he rewarded some loyal, purple-adorned Vikings fans who had cheered for the Purple in the most hostile of circumstances.

"We risked our lives being here!" they shouted at Ryan as he cleaned up the Vikings' bench area after the game. "And we are risking our lives leaving! Please give us a hat!" Feeling sorry for the six true followers of the Men in Purple and what they went through that night, he accommodated each with a Vikings hat, along with a couple of soggy footballs. True Vikings loyalty and spirit must simply be rewarded.

The organization is strong and carries a great tradition with many longtime employees like Bob Hagan, director of public relations. When Hagan talks about the Vikings, he speaks in an honorable tone. He is "Vikings" through and through.

"I grew up here," says Hagan. "We followed the Vikings as a family. If someone called our home during a Vikings game, my mom would answer the phone and politely say, 'Don't you know the Vikings are on television?'

"One day my mom kept me out of school for a doctor appointment. As we drove to the doctor's office, she drove right by," recalls Hagan. "We went to this special event that was being held and Fran Tarkenton was there. He was always my favorite player growing up and our birthdays are the same date."

As a member of the Minnesota Vikings organization, Bob Hagan brings the same enthusiasm he had as a youngster to work with him every day. It is a true dream job fulfilled.

Forty-four years ago and some 200-plus pages back, you were with me when I stepped onto the practice field at the old Midway Stadium in St. Paul and approached Norm Van Brocklin.

Over the course of the last 11 chapters and four and a half decades, we have relived the glorious past of an organizational icon that has the ability to generate great joy or incredible misery all in the span of a few hours.

We have learned about and developed a passion and loyalty for the Minnesota Vikings football team. Better stated, we have paid the dues for entry into the club affectionately known as the Purple Faithful.

And all of this just for the privilege to be able to develop a special bond with the Men who wear the Purple on Sundays in the fall.

From Hall of Fame quarterback Norm Van Brocklin's ferocious desire to win to Bud Grant's steady and calming presence, the faithful have gathered and cheered on the Vikings in all parts of the United States, especially and reverently in the frozen parts of the Northland.

It all began in the ice, wind, sleet, and snow at the old Metropolitan Stadium in Bloomington, Minnesota. The early faithful were there to witness the beginning, the massive destruction of the Chicago Bears in the Purple's first game ever.

"Monsters of the Midway"? Not on that day! It was a day for the Minnesota Vikings: a day when great football players roamed the gridiron in purple apparel, a day when great plans of the Chicago 11 were cast into disarray, a day of infamy for the George Halas band once able to claim championship history of the past.

And when that glorious day ended, a love affair began. It began with a rookie quarterback named Francis Asbury Tarkenton, the son of a preacher who could run and throw the football, bringing crowds to their feet in mass hysteria. It continued with the likes of Tommy Mason, Rip Hawkins, Van Brocklin, and sustained with the pure elegance of the great Hugh McElhenny, who honored us by ending his charming, brilliant career in a purple jersey and helmet adorning horns.

The glory of the early victory didn't last very long, as the pains of an initial franchise in the tough, seasoned, and rugged NFL soon took it's toll on the early lot of rookies and veteran castoffs.

The painful early years were fraught with many losses and were tough on the Dutchman, who was used to winning and things going his way. He thrived on bringing a new team into the NFL and he gave it his best.

Former Viking Larry Bowie, a strong, uncompromising offensive guard from Purdue, played for Van Brocklin for five years and recalls the rugged practices. "We hit every day," says Bowie. "It almost became a 'last man standing' type mentality. According to Bowie, the practices were very "brutal."

Bowie, who has been a longtime operator of Jethro's Char-House and Pub in Mahtomedi, a Twin City suburb, speaks as if it were yesterday when he recalls Van Brocklin's desire to win. It was tough, the practices were long, and those who were there remember.

But The Dutchman was trying his best to formulate a team with players many other teams had no longer wanted on their rosters. It was a tough time, filled with many highs and many lows. Yet, for the Purple faithful, it sure was exciting to be a part of it.

Eventually, some six seasons after the great win over the Chicago Bears, the former Rams and Eagles quarterback had enough and resigned as head coach of the Minnesota Vikings. By then Jim Finks was in control of the team, and he went after an old nemesis from his days in the Canadian Football League, Harry Peter "Bud" Grant.

We knew of the man who arrived to take control of the Purple. We had become familiar with his exploits at the University of Minnesota and as the leader of a group just north of us called the Winnipeg Blue Bombers, known for winning something called the Grey Cup. This was, of course, the equivalent to an NFL championship.

We knew of Grant's athletic prowess while wearing maroon and gold and his reputation as a pretty good football coach in the Canadian ranks. To the Vikings he brought his coaching skills and a desire to win south of the border, as he had done in all aspects of his professional life.

Early in the process, we learned a little about Grant's coaching on the Minnesota sidelines. We learned not to expect to turn the game on after kickoff and glance at Grant's demeanor for an indication of the score. It wasn't going to help. He gave little clue whether the Vikings were ahead by several touchdowns or behind in a game. His sideline antics and stoic approach to consistency have become legendary.

Grant kept it all together for the Vikings and became successful. Never too high and never too low, he was always consistent. And the

Purple won, and they won often—enough for 11 divisional championships and four trips to the Super Bowl.

We became used to Grant. Somehow, we always knew it was going to be all right. If we happened to lose one week, we would prevail the next week. It was just that way. Fred Cox spoke of being behind one game, but said, "I knew we were going to win." Grant was there; he was in control and it was going to be all right.

As the years went on, the faithful became accustomed to winning and got used to what mattered, like divisional titles, conference championships, and Super Bowls.

In 1974, a new face joined the Minnesota Vikings: Mike Lynn. And the 17 years he spent with the team sure were fascinating. His flamboyant management style and the "showbiz" atmosphere he created made attending games enjoyable and reading newspapers' sports sections worthwhile.

With Mike Lynn in charge, something was always going on, from the many newspaper accounts detailing his spending habits to his "barnyard" bantering with Mike Ditka, coach of the Chicago Bears to Elvis almost showing up at a Vikings practice. And it would be remiss to forget his boardroom battles with ownership or the infamous Herschel Walker trade.

Mike Lynn was a businessman and entertainer at heart, and he loved to make things interesting. He was never disappointing in that regard.

It was all a part of Minnesota Vikings football, and we loved it. Mike Lynn was in the front office and Bud Grant was on the field. Coaching came to an end for Grant after 17 beautiful seasons. And then it was all over. Grant's departure hit Purple lovers like a smack upside the head or a devastating block in the back. At first, we couldn't and wouldn't believe it had happened. Grant had retired.

"It was like someone had died," says one lifelong member of the faithful. The reign had come to an end.

The devastating news of Grant's retirement didn't end in a few days or even in a few months. It didn't end with the hiring of a new coach or the beginning of a new season. In fact, the mourning lasted 16 long games, until Mike Lynn decided enough was enough and brought back Grant one last year to restore order to the proud Men of Purple.

So Grant returned, once more bringing credibility to the franchise, and then retired again—this time for good.

Jerry Burns took over as head coach of the Vikings after Grant's final departure and kept the team on track. For the Purple faithful, life seemed to make sense again.

Grant was doing what he loved most, spending time in the woods, on the lakes, and with his family, while "Burnsie" was handling football every Sunday afternoon.

Through the rest of the '80s, the Vikings fared pretty well. The decade brought some exciting teams and great moments. The team was one pass completion from another Super Bowl, management had perceived what would come from the Walker trade, and fans once again saw order return to the franchise.

Mike Lynn left the Vikings in 1991. Jerry Burns left as well after an outstanding career in professional football, 17 years as the offensive coordinator and six as the head coach in Minnesota.

We watched, we read, and we listened to what the future would bring. Grant, Lynn, and Burns were gone, and two-plus decades had passed.

The Vikings ownership group had doubled in size and Roger Headrick, former CEO of the Pillsbury Company, was in charge. He ran the Vikings as a business more so than ever before.

Headrick hired Dennis Green as the new head coach, and the decision was a good one. Green proved to be a solid football coach with many winning and incredibly successful seasons.

He entertained the loyalists with a vertical passing offense designed to throw the ball down the field. With the likes of Cris Carter and Randy Moss, two of the greatest pass receivers of all time, he had all the ingredients to manage it. It was exciting football that brought great seasons and high expectations, but still no Super Bowl.

Although the 1998 Vikings were close, a missed field goal by Gary Anderson, one of the most prolific kickers ever, helped seal their fate in a playoff game at the Metrodome against the Atlanta Falcons.

The Minnesota Vikings had exploded on the NFL scene that year, recording the most productive offense in league history. Randall Cunningham to Carter, Moss, and others was quite a show to witness on Sunday afternoons.

Dennis Green had a good run and brought the Purple many playoff seasons. He left shortly before the end of the 2002 season. Mike Tice came in for four years with some interesting times and some good teams. And now Brad Childress has taken over as the head coach. The present will go on and the future will soon arrive, making more memories and generating more great discussions the next time history is put together.

It seems as though the overall evaluation of the team, however, sometimes takes on a wrong approach. What the organization stands for is also important. Many only look at wins and playoff victories, judging each season as good or bad based on whether the Vikings made the playoffs and advanced to the next round.

Certainly, the sports pages and news coverage focus on such details. So, for 17 weeks in the fall up to the championship game, we read and hear about the wins and the losses, the playoffs, and the Super Bowl. Prior to the season, we are bludgeoned with information on the NFL Draft, mini camps, training camps, and several weeks of meaningless preseason games. That is just the way it is, and most true fans follow carefully. For some of the faithful, maybe the scores are all that matter, but for others, hopefully the organization itself and what it has stood for through the years magnify what is really important.

Brad Madson and his devoted work in the community is a Super Bowl victory every week. Whether giving out dictionaries to third graders, visiting sick children at hospitals, shopping for Christmas presents with underprivileged youth, or playing bingo at a veterans home, the Vikings are community leaders and winners.

Brad Childress may have had a six-win season his first year at the helm, but he continues to gain victories in other ways. The time Childress spent with Chad Knapp and others will stay with them a lifetime. As Brad Childress has said, "You are judged by your ability to win." But taking time from a busy schedule to discuss football plays with a young boy represents a different kind of success.

No question that winning the Super Bowl in professional football is important. It is what every player, coach, scout, and team employee strives for from the first day of training camp. But the personalities within the organization, who they are and what they have meant to both the community and to the fans, are what make the Vikings significant.

The Purple faithful remember the old Metropolitan Stadium and the cold memorable and deplorable weather conditions. We remember the frozen field without heaters and gloves.

We followed The Dutchman and marveled at the finesse of the great Fran Tarkenton, along with the stamina and toughness of Mick Tingelhoff, Jim Marshall, and Bill Brown. And what hasn't already been said about Bud Grant, Jim Finks, Jeff Diamond, and Mike Lynn? There have been many others, including Les Steckel, Jerry Burns, Dennis Green, Roger Headrick, Red McCombs, Mike Tice, the Wilfs, and Brad Childress. Max Winter and the ownership of 10. Osborn, Page, and Eller. Krause, Foreman, Browner, Voigt, and Yary. Studwell, Alderman, Hilgenberg, and many, many more. We remember all who have worn the Purple.

And we cannot forget the men behind the Vikings who have often been responsible for putting it all together on Sundays, like Paul Wiggin, Frank Gilliam, and Jerry Reichow.

Wiggin, one of the nicest people ever according to many, has used his wealth of professional expertise to help build the Vikings. A coach, player, evaluator, and a great person, he has served many roles with the franchise for two decades. He understands the game and he knows what it takes to win.

"I never had a day in my career when I didn't look forward to going to work," say Wiggin. "I have always had the greatest respect for the Minnesota Vikings franchise."

What about Frank Gilliam, a traveling and scouting genius who has worked for the Vikings for three decades? A master at evaluating talent and networking across the nation, he has been instrumental behind the scenes of some of the Vikings' most successful college drafts. Gilliam's longtime association with the team began before he actually became a Viking, when he played for future Vikings coach Bud Grant in the Canadian Football League.

Jerry Reichow's history is unmatched with the Purple. Acquired by the Vikings in 1961, he has been with the team in various capacities for over 46 years and connected to the NFL since 1956, when he was drafted by the Detroit Lions.

New to the Purple's front office working closely with Brad Childress is Rick Spielman, who comes with a great reputation for knowing and loving the game. His organizational skills and attention to detail give him a solid understanding of his role as vice president of player personnel.

With a background that includes the Bears, Lions, and Dolphins, Spielman comes well prepared to build for the Vikings a positive future. He knows what it takes to be successful in the NFL and plans to bring his knowledge to the Vikings as the process of paving a road to the Super Bowl begins.

Behind the glory, we learned about Brad Madson, Bob Hagan, Dan Endy, Ryan, and Zamberletti. Since the beginning, great players, coaches, and staff have made the Minnesota Vikings franchise into an organizational icon, an NFL leader, and a leader in life.

And finally, we've come to know people like Matt Birk, a person first and a player second. Through his life off the field, Birk epitomizes what is right about great athletes and the Minnesota Vikings. Birk is truly a great player, a perennial Pro Bowler, and the cornerstone of Vikings pride in a positive way. "Not a lot of people get to do this," says Birk. "It is a privilege driving to work to do what I do. Sometimes I can't believe it. It is hard for me to get used to what I do for a living. I'm not Matt Birk the pro football player, I'm just Matt Birk, the chubby, freckle-faced kid."

Every picture of Matt Birk seen on walls of the Purple faithful, in football locker rooms and arenas, and inside newspapers or magazines brings pride to the Purple and truly represents the tradition, dignity, and honor of the Minnesota Vikings organization.

The historic wins and the devastating losses will always be there, and many more will come in the future. But there will also be more stories to tell as the Minnesota Vikings continue to meet high expectations on the field and connect to those off the field.

Kernal Buhler worked in many capacities in his 18 years with the Vikings. He feels strongly that the community makes a person "feel responsible" to do good things for others. The Vikings have done just that through the development of their Children's Fund, setting a model other professional sports organizations have followed. "It was the first of its kind," says Buhler. "It was the first in organizing a way of giving."

Buhler had many wonderful years with the Vikings and speaks of the organization's commitment to the community with great pride. Purple players, coaches, and team personnel have been a major part of the Minnesota area for almost a half-century. Their commitment to integrity, credibility, and gracious giving to those in need is worthy of the highest of recognition and admiration.

The state of Minnesota and the surrounding region has truly embraced this organization over the past 46 years, and for good reason. As Fred Zamberletti, legendary mentor to many, reflects back on his glorious 46 years with the franchise and all he has experienced, he quietly says, "I have received more than I have ever given."

I hope that, over the past 11 chapters and four decades of Minnesota Vikings glory, you have enjoyed the ride. I know I sure have! This has been *A TRADITION OF PURPLE.*

# INDEX

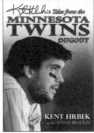